The Mother-in-Law's MANUAL

PROVEN STRATEGIES FOR CREATING AND
MAINTAINING HEALTHY RELATIONSHIPS
WITH MARRIED CHILDREN

bright sky press

2365 Rice Blvd., Suite 202 Houston, Texas 77005

10   9   8   7   6   5   4   3   2   1

Library of Congress Cataloging-in Publication Data
Lieberman, Susan Abel.
The Mother-in-law's manual : proven strategies for creating and maintaining healthy
relationships with married children / Susan Abel Lieberman.
p. cm.
ISBN 978-1-933979-47-2 (jacketed hardcover : alk. paper)
— ISBN 978-1-933979-41-0 (softcover : alk. paper)
1. Mothers-in-law—Family relationships. 2. Daughters-in-law—Family relationships.
3. Mothers-in-law—Psychology. 4. Interpersonal relations. I. Title.

HQ759.25.L54 2009
646.7'8—dc22

2009000313

Book and cover design by Cregan Design
Illustrations by Mike Guillory
Edited by Hillary Durgin Harmon

Printed in China through Asia Pacific Offset

www.motherinlawsmanual.com

The Mother-in-Law's MANUAL

SUSAN ABEL LIEBERMAN, PH.D.

bright sky press
HOUSTON, TEXAS

Introduction

❧

T his book owes a deep debt to all the women who shared their
stories, revealed their hopes and disappointments, and
who described very personal feelings. It was a joy to talk with
people all over the country who are trying to be good mothers-in-
law. I also enjoyed the more informal conversations with sons,
daughters, and their spouses who gave different perspectives. I
learned so much from the people who were kind enough to talk with
me and hope those who read this book will share in that learning.

The Mother-in-Law's Manual grew out of my own desire to forge strong
and satisfying adult relationships with my children and their
spouses. Sometimes, I feel I am not doing such a good job. How
comforting it has been to find that I am not alone in my feelings
or my hopes, and that my own shortcomings and fears are shared
by others.

Although I feel enormous appreciation for the many people who
helped me figure out what to write, there are two reasons I cannot
thank them by name. I don't know the names of all of them.
Sometimes, we chatted in airport lounges or in doctors' offices.
Where I do know names and have notes, I have promised confi-
dentiality. Almost every mother-in-law I interviewed wanted to be
sure she would not be named or recognizable in the book. So, with
the exception of a few dear friends, there are no names here of the
people who are quoted but lots of gratitude.

There are a few friends who I do want to recognize by name
because they were especially supportive when I was still unsure
if I really had a book. They read the early drafts, made excellent
comments, and gave me the encouragement I needed. Judith
Grossman cheered me on from before word one made it to the
paper and continued to offer her wisdom and red editing pen
long after it seemed reasonable to ask her for more. Kathleen
Sullivan offered publishing support and expertise from the start.
And Dick Goldberg's thumbs up mattered. Madeleine Appel, Sue

Cejka, Jennifer Chiu, and Barbara Rosen kept my spirits up and improved both my thinking and my writing. Dale and Tom Baker, Ravelle Brickman, Ruth Brodsky, Roberta Diddel, Amy Lawch, Dorothy Mahan, Barbara Marwell, and Michele Anne Simms all read and commented on drafts. A special word of thanks to Christine Adams whose warmth and insights always delight and enlighten me. There are many others whose friendship and wisdom kept me optimistic and grounded. You know—I hope you know—who you are, how much I value having you as friends, and how much a few encouraging words over lunch or coffee matter. Deborah Tannen and Nora Ephron are not people I have ever met, but their books also encouraged and educated me.

It was great good fortune that my friend Nancy Rust urged me to "talk to the publisher down the hall." I was not looking for a regional publishing house, but finding Bright Sky and the three terrific and knowledgeable women who run it was a great gift. I have only appreciation and admiration for Ruina Wallace Judd, Lucy Herring Chambers, and Ellen Peeples Cregan. Having Hillary Durgin Harmon work with me as an editor certainly made this a better book. Ladies, champagne and strawberries for you all!

My sons and their wives have my love and admiration. I did not believe writing this book would be difficult for my children and their spouses. There is, I thought, no cause for worry because I see them as smart, kind, thoughtful people who are generous and considerate with me. It was out of my own sense of inadequacy in building stronger relationships that I was led to look more closely at the mother-in-law challenge.

In the moment, I'm not sure speaking publicly strengthened my relationships with these young women, but I hold the belief that in time, this will take us all to a more loving, more understanding place. It is no simple thing to have your mother or mother-in-law talk about family relationships publicly. Let me make clear to all that my daughters-in-law are very good women! They make our sons deliciously happy, and this book is not about them. It is about me and about the issues with which mothers-in-law—even those lucky enough to know their daughters-in law are smart, kind, and thoughtful—sometimes find themselves struggling.

While this book focuses on being a mother and mother-in-law, it does not imply that fathers and fathers-in-law are unimportant. For me, my husband Michael is my anchor. He helps me stay grounded, lets me sound off when I need it, and loves all of us with an intensity that warms us deeply.

The stories in this book are, to the best of my knowledge, true. Names and details have been altered to provide privacy for the many people who spoke so candidly. On some occasions, I have blended people's words when they spoke about similar things. The quoted words are rarely exact quotes but usually reconstructions from my memory and my notes. Always, I have aimed to be true to the tone and the intent of the person speaking. In very few instances, stories came to me second or third hand.

Writing is a great clarifier. Writing this book helped me understand my feelings about being the mother of adults and the mother-in-law of the lovely women our sons married. I hope it helps others as well, because more love and less hurt can only be good for us and for the world. 🐾

Susan Abel Lieberman
Houston, Texas

In memory of
my mother-in-law,
Rita Williams Lieberman,
1920 — 2001

I could do better now.

Table of Contents

CHAPTER ONE

Dr. Spock, I Still Need You

WHEREAS KNOWLEDGE IS SOMETHING WE HAVE,
WISDOM IS SOMETHING WE BECOME.

– Frances Vaughn and Roger Walsh

I am forever grateful to Dr. Spock and all those other parenting experts whose insights helped us raise our children. But I want to tell them that they stopped the developmental cycles too soon. They didn't warn me that our children's marriage was yet another stage of development in the child-rearing journey for which we parents could use some guidance.

Long before I was pregnant, I planned to be an excellent mother and have lovely children. Postpregnancy, it quickly became apparent that there was a gap between wishing and executing. It took cargo loads of advice to figure out what made sense for my husband and me as we muddled through and got the babes out of diapers and into school, past fighting about the merits of bike helmets, through adolescent recalcitrance, beyond the demands of college tuition bills. Miracle of miracles, time came when they could not only buy a car without assistance, they could also pay for it.

While it took decades of focused attention to be able to write that last paragraph, the happy bottom line is that our boys grew into kind, responsible men. I thought the difficult times were behind us. The most trying decisions now would be what restaurant to choose for dinner and what time to get there.

I had no idea that there was an entire new learning curve waiting just around the corner—the mother-in-law challenge. I knew that parenting would be demanding, but it never occurred to me to think my sons' marrying would bring its own challenges. Where is Dr. Spock on this stage of development?

Was I being arrogant when I unconsciously assumed that any people our children would marry would be delighted to have me as a mother-in-law? I also assumed that they would find my husband and me kind, interesting, bright, and helpful. If they loved our offspring, wouldn't they also love us? And if our children loved them, wouldn't we think they were great?

Hmmm. That was, I now see, a bit of an overblown assumption. It caught me by surprise to realize that the way it often works is that the child you raised from a burping babe—whose every eye twitch you can interpret, who has been hand crafted by you into a fully sustaining human being and is now actually an interesting dinner partner—brings home a *stranger* and says, "Oh, by the way, we are getting married."

He or she is going to merge with this *other* person. Daughters who bring home future husbands and sons who bring home future wives are introducing a foreign agent into the family mix. Men who bring home men and women who bring home women can make the situation still more complicated, but the underlying issues are the same. There is no telling who will be easily assimilated and who will trigger disruption. Even if you have known these people for years, have watched them in the sixth grade pageant, have seen them dressed for the prom, have applauded their college graduation, you most likely don't really know them *yet*. Up until now, they wanted to be sure you liked them. Now you need to be sure they like you.

Our own children can metamorphose from cuddlers to curmudgeons. "I used to cut the crusts off my son's peanut butter sandwiches," reminisces one mother. "I'm not sure when he started being a stranger who speaks to me as if we just met at a board meeting." Being a mother-in-law is not only about relating to the person our child marries. It is also about relating to our children when they begin to form their own distinct families that may not replicate our values.

Maybe it is like being a term-limited monarch. We are always The Mother, but our reign has run its course, and policy and procedures have passed to a new administration. We may get to sit on the Council of Advisors, appreciated for our grasp of history, but we are no longer considered the highest authority.

There are advantages to giving up full-time parental responsibilities, but some of us want to hang on to our familiar roles. As I listen to mothers-in-law, their children, and their children's partners, it is clear that it isn't always sweetness and light. What gets in the way?

Well, the most prevalent choice is—imagine this—*them*. We mothers-in-law, I can tell you, live in the land of the righteous and just. Our children and their spouses, they are all over the map.

Each generation says thank you to the past generation by investing in the next generation. Our children don't owe us anything—in spite of the times we want to shout, "Do you remember what I did for *you*!"—but that doesn't mean we have no expectation, or they have no obligation. We want things for our children and also from our children.

Mothers say, "Oh, I just want them to be happy." Yes, but honestly, don't we want more? I love seeing our two sons in love and contented. It is a lot. But it is not enough, at least not for me. I want to feel loved by them and their families. I want to be a part of their lives. I want communications to be easy and respectful. I want us to all have a sense of ease and openness when we are together. And I want time together. I pray my children find contentment ... and that I do as well.

I want a great deal ... and so do most mothers. The voice of a normally cheerful sixty-three-year-old woman is shadowed by pain when she explains the tensions she feels being in her daughter and son-in-law's house. "I don't know if it is the fact that my son-in-law comes from a very different cultural background, or that my daughter doesn't have a sense of humor, but we see the world differently, make different choices, have different child-rearing philosophies, and, damn, it's hard. It isn't what I imagined for us." This woman makes her peace with having less ease in the relationship than she wants, as many women do, but it's not a first choice. She makes a comment that I am to hear repeated dozens of times: "I always feel like I'm walking on eggs." Months later, I tell this to one of my sons. "But Mom," he says, "we walk on eggs too."

The question that grabs me, is what can we learn that will help us navigate this egg-walking adult stage of child-rearing? As I was able to learn how to parent for the most part successfully, is it possible to learn to deal successfully with being the mother of married men and women and the mother-in-law of their spouses? This book springs from my own determined efforts to be a successful mother-in-law, which also means being a successful mother of my adult children. I have talked with dozens of women and read scores of books as part of this exploration, but much of this is my own experience laid out for others to look at and say, "Yup, that makes sense," or, "That seems really dumb to me. I see that it would be better to do ..." I have learned a great deal from other women over coffee as well as from my own children and their partners. I like the learning. I know it will continue because I am the better for it, and I hope I can contribute to others who also want to learn. ❧

CHAPTER TWO

What We Expect Influences What We Get

WE ARE DISTURBED NOT BY WHAT HAPPENS TO US,
BUT BY OUR THOUGHTS ABOUT WHAT HAPPENS.

– Epictetus

Reading from Scripts Written with Invisible Ink

So many mature women who have worked hard to become self-confident, grounded adults feel off balance when they find themselves feeling put out, put off, or put down in their role of mother or mother-in-law. A freelance writer in New York has two married sons, one in another city, and one in another country. "It's not my daughter-in-law, it's my son who seems totally committed to putting me down at every turn," she says. "Why does he do this to me, to his children, to his family? They want to like me, and he can neither discuss what digs at him nor give it up." A sensible, open-hearted photographer in Houston feels hurt by a son-in-law who somehow thinks his wife's mother is competing with him. For a lawyer in California, it's a daughter-in-law who ignores her and makes her feel unwanted and useless. Certainly, there are many women like the high-powered and hard-driving company president who is not gentle in her business assessments but has only the most joyous comments about her sons and their wives. "I love the women my sons married, and they are warm and generous with me. It's a pleasure to spend time with them." But, in talking randomly with women of all ages, stages, and backgrounds, this contentment is not so easy to find.

It is not impossible. Many women have good things to say about their children and their spouses. When I am talking with one of these women, I always ask, "Why do you think it is so easy for you when many women have difficulty?" The answers are most often something about expectations: "I don't expect anything ... I just love unconditionally ... Hey, it is their life now, and my opinion doesn't matter ... Well, it is my job to live my life and their job to live theirs ... My role isn't to have opinions but to cheer them on in whatever they want to do."

Yet, for more women, being a mother-in-law is often a difficult role. We often get hurt—and inadvertently cause hurt. No one wants this. What we all want, regardless of where we are in the generational hierarchy, is to feel loved and respected. What is required to unleash those particular emotional states, however, is often not so clear.

I think the starting place has got to be figuring out our own expectations. That mother-anthem, "I just want them to be happy!" needs to be deconstructed. We may not realize we have notions about what our children and their partners need to do to find this happiness—but it turns out we usually do. We may not tune into our own visions until we find events are not unfolding as we have imagined them in our heads.

In the face of such conflict, there is no Court of Visions to rule on what is "right," no set of family best practices, or most reasonable expectations that we can consult. We need to go digging into the mostly unarticulated—and often unrecognized—expectations we carry to the wedding when our children marry. We have a script. It isn't written down. We don't speak it. We may not admit it exists. We may not even be aware that it exists. It exists!

I met an impressively chic woman who wore great shoes and beautiful jewelry. Her figure wasn't perfect, but her clothes fit her so well and were so lovely that it was easy to miss the imperfections. I wished she could take me shopping and was surprised when I found out how much her daughter-in-law wanted the opposite.

> Before my children were married, I so wanted to build a relationship with the young woman who would soon be our daughter-in-law. She is very attractive but doesn't dress well. I have a great sense of style and love to shop. I thought we could meet in New York and go shopping together, and it would be fun, and she'd come away with a trousseau—all these great new clothes that I was thrilled to be able to buy. It never occurred to me that this would make her hugely uncomfortable. She doesn't like to shop. She certainly didn't want my judgment about her style, and having me buy things for her felt really odd to her. I think I am reasonably perceptive, but I missed all of that. Luckily, my son and I have a good relationship, and he had to sit me down and say, "Look, Mom, you are setting yourself—and me—up for trouble."

Fortunately, she is perceptive, and she got it. She understood that wanting this young woman to like what this mother liked was not a great strategy. Instead, she slowed down and let the relationship grow into friendship over time. "Honestly, I hate how she dresses. But she makes my son happy. She is a happy person. They have a good life. Her tastes don't seem to affect her life, so I understand this is my problem and I have to let it go … let it go … let it go …"

A young couple told me how a generous offer by her parents to buy them a house caused hours of argument between the young woman and her new husband. The parents assumed the couple would stay in their hometown and live in their neighborhood. It is what the parents wanted, and so they decided to help make it possible. The young husband and wife were not ready to lock into such important decisions, but the economics of the deal were seductive. And so good intentions, based on a preconceived script, had bad results. In order not to look ungrateful and to escape the confusion caused by such directed generosity, the young couple put increasing distance between themselves and her parents. They didn't want to say yes, and they didn't want to say no, and they didn't know how to say something else. What the parents thought was generosity, the children felt was meddling.

The Shame/Blame Trap

Discussions of emerging work in neuroscience help me make some sense out of my own behavior. The research tells us more and more about how important the mind-body connection is and how what we think shapes what we do. Do you recall watching the Summer Olympics on TV? Do you remember the high divers? They climb the ladder, walk out onto the edge of the diving board, and then just stand there for a bit, not moving, while a couple of million people watch and wait. Why do they do this?

They are, it seems, visioning the perfect dive, seeing themselves turn and arc and cut cleanly into the water, so that their bodies will hold that picture and automatically execute the vision. Picturing the actions we want to take helps to make them real. We can do this positively or negatively. I can picture myself going to the gym and being strong and disciplined, and it helps me get there.

Or I can think about the box of chocolate truffles in the fridge in the garage that I'm not going to touch, and next thing I know, a truffle is in my mouth.

If we think our daughter-in-law will love cooking with us, and she hates to cook, if we think our son-in-law will be more than willing to update the plumbing and he is wrench-adverse, if we think our children will welcome us into their new lives and they get lost in themselves, there is a sense of betrayal, even if the deal was never discussed. If we think that being a mother-in-law will be easy and that all will go well, and then it does not, we are disappointed and, perhaps, surprised. Sometimes we are hurt or angry. We develop a story about what happened that is self-protecting because, most often, our first impulse is to blame someone else when we believe we are acting from good intentions. The new daughter-in-law is jealous of our son's affection, the son-in-law resentful of our ability to offer gifts. Or our own children have been sabotaged, distracted, seduced. I am sure, from dozens of interviews, that most of the stories do not identify us as the problem.

Dr. Brené Brown, a professor of social work at the University of Houston, does research on the emotion of shame. Brown defines shame as "the intensely painful feeling or experience of believing we are flawed and therefore unworthy of acceptance and belonging." When the children we love and want so much for reject our desire to connect, or they feel rejected by us, it is a shame trigger. When we feel shame, that awful wash of inadequacy, Brown notes that we often mask it with anger. We all know those moments when we started out trying to say something we thought was important in a calm and nonjudgmental way, met sticky resistance, and ended up blowing the whole conversation.

We may lash out by blaming and finding fault. Most often the result is more deeply ruptured relationships, when our intention from the start was to have a good relationship. Brown writes:

> Anger is not a "bad" emotion. In fact, feeling anger
> and appropriately expressing anger are vital to rela-
> tionship building. Lashing out at others when we

are in shame is not about "feeling anger." When we are doing this, we feel shame and mask it with anger. Furthermore, shame-motivated anger and blame are rarely expressed in a constructive way. Shame floods us with emotion and pain and the shame/blame/anger instinct is to pour it all over someone else. If one of our primary shame screens is anger and blame, it is essential that we understand and acknowledge this coping strategy. Next, we need to find out how, when we recognize that we are in shame, to calm down and stay mindful.[1]

If we expect all will go well and it doesn't, we want to blame someone else for the disappointment. Maybe a "someone else" is contributing to the problem, but odds are it is out of his or her own sense of wanting not to feel any shame. Instead of expecting all good things, what if we just expect that it may be difficult? What if we expect that we will have to grow and learn a bit ourselves in the process?

Isn't this how we managed the travails of parenthood? If we truly expected our babies would immediately smile, gurgle, lock into a schedule, and quickly sleep through the night, we would likely have returned them all in no time flat.

Marriage as an Immigration Problem

As I worked though all these thoughts about in-lawing, I found myself comparing marriage to immigration. When two adults come together to form a new family, each is migrating to a new country, the country of Other, where the habits and cultural norms, and maybe the food and even the language, are different. Each must do what immigrants do—decide when and how much to assimilate. Because the difficulties that might arise are smoothed over by new love, and because the couple usually expects that they will work things out, the couple can have an easier time than their parents who are just along for the ride. Just as older immigrants may remain unassimilated while their children merge cultures without a thought, so may parents find themselves reluctant to adapt to unanticipated circumstances. We know that immigrant children can feel ashamed of parental habits when these are exposed to others. Maybe our children sometimes find themselves a little embarrassed when they have to explain family-of-origin habits to a new spouse who is going, "Huh ... why do they do *that*?"

We didn't sign up for changes in our cultural habits. We have worked hard to make sense of our lives, and they are working just fine, thank you. Not only are we less ready for change; such change, neurologically, is more difficult for us than it is for younger immigrants because our brain plasticity does decline as we age, making it harder to respond to new patterns. Our children may not be making it up when they tell us we are acting "old." Dr. Norman Doidge is a psychiatrist, psychoanalyst, researcher, author, essayist, and poet. He has written an intriguing and accessible book called *The Brain That Changes Itself,* in which the current work in neuroplasticity is explained so that nonscientists like me can understand it. Doidge writes:

> We find familiar types of stimulation pleasurable; we seek out like-minded individuals to associate with, and research shows we tend to ignore or forget or attempt to discredit information that does not match our beliefs, or perception of the world, because it is very distressing and difficult to think and perceive in unfamiliar ways. Increasingly the aging individual acts to preserve the structures within, and when there is a mismatch between his internal neurocognitive structures and the world, he seeks to change the world. In small ways he begins to micromanage his environment, to control it and make it familiar.[2]

But if this part of the research inclines us to throw up our hands and say, "Okay, don't ask this old dog to learn any new tricks," newer research tells us the dog doesn't get off so easily. We've got ample capacity for learning even as we age. When people change cultures, even well into adulthood, they learn to perceive in a new way. There is all sorts of talk in the media about U.S. citizens expecting new immigrants to get with the American program. We see that some do this with greater facility than others. Our hard wiring plays a part—but so does attitude.

What if our own culture taught us that when our children marry, we were expected to undergo a cultural learning experience—and that, in fact, it was something to look forward to because it did good things to our rigidifying brain.

Often, we hear older people talk about how being with young people helps them to stay young and engaged. What if the very challenges presented to us by our adult children were, in fact, one of the ways to keep exercising our brains and keeping them plastic? "There is an endless war of nerves going on inside each of our brains," Doidge explains. "If we stop exercising our mental skills, we do not just forget them; the brain map space for those skills is turned over to the skills we practice instead."[3] In other words, let our brains get lazy, and learning gets even harder. We could take up bridge or beading or tango dancing as a way of practicing new learning. But our adult children can also lead us to learn new things and uncover new ways of seeing the world. Just think ... our most perplexing in-laws might actually be a secret weapon in flexible brainpower.

This is not easy behavior on many levels. First, breaking old habits is tough. If we think a certain way or behave a certain way reflexively, wishing the habit away is insufficient. "When we try to break a bad habit, we think the solution is to put something new into the container. But when we learn a bad habit, it takes over a brain map, and each time we repeat it, it claims more control of that map and prevents the use of that space for the 'good' habits."[4]

The key to change is mindfulness. If we are mindful about what annoys us, we wire that into the brain. If we decide we can't stand it when our daughter does that fake laugh, we'll hear it all the time. It isn't helpful to be constantly alert to things that upset or hurt us. If, instead, we can focus on new behavior, our own new behavior, and think about it carefully, we, amazingly, create new brain maps.

For example, telling myself each day how much I dislike going to the gym only reinforced my dislike of the gym. It's much better that I tell myself each day that I can and will go to the gym, and I'm a terrific person for having the determination to do this good thing, and in time I know I will come to value the benefits. To convert my couch-potato self into a regular gym-goer, I had to spend lots of time and attention talking to myself and coaching my reluctant body out the door and into the gym. No, I have not mutated into an athlete, and I still look for excuses to skip the gym, but I go much more now than ever before, and my funny brain seems to give me more trouble when I skip than when I go.

So, instead of thinking, again and again, that a particular son or daughter-in-law lacks qualities we favor, which will only serve to make the poor soul seem more inadequate to us, we have got to put a different message in place and focus on thinking the new message enough until it becomes wired into our brain. We might be mindful of how much he or she worries about appearing incompetent to us, or how much this person fears not being in control, and be mindful of what we might do to ease the discomforts. I never had an expectation that being a mother-in-law would require hard mental work, but even with two generous and talented daughters-in-law, I'm mindful of it now.

When we change countries, states, neighborhoods, or jobs, it's easy for us to figure out that we have got to stop saying, "But they did it this way when I was ..." We don't stop feeling part of our native country or state, and maybe we hold great admiration and affection for our old neighborhood or workplace. Certainly, we want to bring the best of those places with us to share, but we also adapt. We aren't moving to a new family when our children marry—but they are, both of them, the husband and wife. It isn't her moving to his family or him moving to her family. They are moving to a new country that they will create together. Yes, we get territorial. Use *my* bill of rights. Celebrate *my* holidays. Serve *my* food. Even if we don't see it like a competition, we are likely to consider each deviation a loss.

Remembering the Lessons of Gardening

Decades ago, when I began interviewing for my first job, I was told that I needed a good answer to the question, "What is your worst fault?" The answer I chose was impatience. I chose it both because it was true, and I hoped it would make me seem like a go-getter, a person who was going to jump in and do the work. I told people who asked that my worst fault and best strength were the same. In my youthful wisdom, I thought my impatience more virtue than vice. I don't think that any longer. I separate the desire to accomplish and to see results from the ability to wait until the pump is primed, the moment is right, the data is in, the action is considered. In other words, I'm more grown-up at sixty-five than twenty-five. Would that I were more grown-up still.

I did not look at my baby and expect he would never sleep through the night or be toilet trained. I did look at my daughters-in-law and think: "Well, this is it." But it isn't. The newly beloved has to get comfortable with our child, with us, with the idea of being married, with the responsibilities of creating a new household. If our children and their partners are still in their early twenties, they may not even be finished wiring in their own brain, let alone making sense of ours. We've got to be as patient with growing relationships as we are with growing gardens ... planting, fertilizing, watering, weeding, sometimes replanting, pruning. I always want what I plant to bloom instantly. It doesn't usually work that way.

By the time our sons were grown, I had made so many mistakes, there was no counting. It might have been better to have known more about parenting—and gardening—before I started, but it took experience, not just theory, to help me understand the events on the ground. I saw that I had to work on myself to work on our kids. I had to change some of what I believed was going to be the right thing to think or the right way to behave. I had to be patient and wait for what we were teaching to take hold.

I can't go back and do it better, but it is useful to recall and review what I learned. One big lesson is that things don't stay the same. Situations change, we change, they change, the relationship changes. If a relationship is not great at the start, we still have to be reliable, loving, and consistent right from the beginning. My good fortune is that I had Drs. Benjamin Spock and Berry Brazelton and dozens of other gurus to help me figure out what to do when I started parenting. Who helps when we start in-lawing? Who says, "Look, this is a whole new developmental stage, and it takes some figuring out?"

When our son first introduced me to the young woman he had met in his dorm and started dating, I could not imagine how happy they would be as husband and wife, or what a wonderful addition she would become to our family.

It took me a couple of years to feel really at ease with this woman. It took her a couple of years to open up to me. Is it perfect? I am not sure what perfect would look like, and sure, there are things I don't have in our good relationship that I would like, but there is so much I do have. I suspect I do things that she would prefer I don't do. But we have been committed to making our relationship healthy, to bonding as a family … and it works … works well. She invites me into their lives; I'm deeply appreciative.

I now know I was misguided to assume that I would immediately love the people my children chose to marry. With the wisdom of hindsight, it makes sense that they might seek out qualities I don't provide. Certainly, I married a man different from my own father and different from me. As I look from a distance, I suspect one reason our younger son is so attracted to his wife is in part for the ways she is different from his mother. She seems to have avoided my most difficult characteristics, and I can imagine our son finds this enormously relaxing.

This daughter-in-law, whose sense of privacy and reserve make me reluctant even to write about her, taught me that I must wait for her to walk us into a relationship. It is our job to fall in love with her because our son fell in love with her. A wise woman in her eighties with four well-married children counsels that mothers need to be patient. "When the son with whom I am closest first married, his wife winced when I hugged him in front of her. Thirty years later, I have a different and much better relationship with her. It just takes time to get to know one another and become trusting."

It took my own mother more than a decade to "get" my husband's humor. Now, I think if we split up, she might choose him over me. I am ashamed to say that I don't think I understood my own mother-in-law until after she died. I used to get irritated by her inability to speak her mind. Everything was always fine, wonderful, just right. She wouldn't even commit to whether she preferred coffee or tea but was happy to have "Whatever you are having." Now, too late, I understand that what she was really thinking was, "I just don't want any conflict or to make any waves. I want to make your life easy in a way that my mother never helped me make mine easy, so don't let me cause you any trouble." She had learned, from her life's experiences, to use an indirect form of communication. I, who so value the direct, assumed mine was the correct way. I feel such sadness for not appreciating her very kind intention.

Another woman with regrets reflects on how self-absorbed she was, first with law school and then with building her career. "My mother-in-law was a very nice woman. She was always kind to me. I didn't appreciate her when she was alive. It took so much of my energy to manage my own life that I kind of skipped over the fact that she was leading a life too. I deeply regret now not letting her know how much I appreciated who she was."

This is embarrassing to admit, but in some part of my less rational self, I expect everything I say will be heard as helpful and loving and understood just as it is meant. If not ridiculous, it is simply impossible. In fact, I need to expect that there will be misunderstandings. Since I misunderstand, why would it not happen that I am misunderstood? I should not be surprised ... or hurt ... or defensive. Short of that—which is quite far from my personal state of maturity at the moment—the misunderstandings are just weeds that have to be uprooted.

We can uproot them by communicating with our children but also by finding ways to reconstruct our view of what is happening. A friend of mine was catching me up about her family. "You know Max is engaged," she said of her grandson. "Do you like the young woman?" I asked. "Well, yes I like her, but I am bothered by her insensitivities." Here is what that meant: Max and his fiancée, who both are in graduate school in New Jersey, went to visit his parents in upstate Massachusetts. They didn't arrive until late Saturday evening, tired, and were leaving on Monday. On Sunday, they got up and went to church until almost noon. The young man's parents are not Christians. The young woman, who is the daughter of a minister, set as a condition of marriage that children be raised in her faith, and her fiancé has been going to church with her for about a year. Max's parents felt abandoned, hurt that going to church took time away from family. Such an obvious statement about religion underscored for them the pain of seeing their son leave their faith. My friend, the grandmother, reinforced her own son and daughter-in-law's annoyance with this young woman, the "insensitive" young woman. Yet it is Max who knows his family, who is bringing his girl to his house, who should understand his parents. If the family needed to question judgment, why focus on the young woman? Why not on their son? While this family thought spending several hours in church during a short visit was thoughtless, is it possible the young woman assumed she would seem irresponsible not to go to church? That is how it would have been interpreted in her own family. It is so challenging to remember that there can be multiple perspectives.

I was told a story about a woman with Parkinson's disease that made me think about how it is to meet a mother-in-law for the first time after illness has struck her. The new addition to the family only knows this person in her ill state. There are no memories when sickness did not shape behavior. The woman with Parkinson's, for example, is unable to establish herself in her relationship with either her daughter-in-law or son-in-law as the healthy, vital, energetic person her children knew her to be. Neither does she have as much energy nor as much time to put into building a relationship. She must rely more on her own children to help her build an adult relationship with their spouses. What should she expect from her children and their partners? What happens when she expects more care and concern than they offer? Who must change?

Think Structurally, Not Personally

When I feel hurt or insulted, it helps me to remember something from the years spent teaching leadership at a local university. I would tell my students that one reason leadership is hard is that we think personally when we would do better to think structurally. Most of what happens really isn't all about us. People act the way they do because of who they are in the context of where they are. They are almost always more focused on taking care of their own needs than thinking about how they can make us happy or unhappy. It is more useful to ask what can we do to change the dynamic of what is happening than to fret over why can't we get someone to carry out our wishes. One woman talked about how it bothered her that one of her daughters-in-law never communicated with her directly. And then this woman suddenly saw that she also communicated with her son and did not include his wife or go directly to her, even on decisions she knew were the young woman's to make. "I shifted. She shifted. It isn't a big shift, but it's progress."

Reading, talking, and thinking about what is going on helps us act more constructively. We mothers-in-law need each other now just as we did when the kids were little and we swapped information, complaints, fears, hopes. Oddly, it seemed easier to admit I felt inadequate as a mother than to admit I wasn't sure I was doing so well in the mother-in-law category. Sensibly, we want to slide away from conflict and disagreement. "I want to have a nice life, so it's not worth getting upset," explained a woman in Tennessee. "She still has her hormones and I don't. I was much easier to tip over, but now that I am older, I let more things slide and pick my battles." Still, this woman feels she is in competition with her daughter-in-law's mother and is always going to come up on the short end. "My daughter-in-law is a perfectionist, and I see she wants to please me, but that actually makes for more conflict. If I say anything, she feels criticized, and I get blamed."

There are parallels between raising the kids and relating to them after they marry. A woman who took lots of parenting classes remembers lessons from the book *I'm Okay, You're Okay*, where parents were taught to make *I* statements not *you* statements. We learned not to say, "You never pick up your toys," but rather, "Mommy likes it very much when you pick up your toys before dinner." Same with a husband and the underwear on the bathroom floor. It worked, she recalls, "… so now I am saying to my new daughter-in-law, 'I so appreciate it when you let me know when it works well for you to visit, and if you can do this well in advance, it helps me juggle our crazy schedule,' rather than 'You make it so difficult to communicate around plans.'"

Understanding the different ways we process information and make decisions helps to avoid being judgmental about the different ways we manage our lives.

Some of us arrive at closure slowly, while others are quick to process and decide. The first group likes to keep options open. The second group wants to settle things and move on. These are just different ways of being in the world, but it can be tempting for us to make negative judgments about each other. In chapter 6, this is explored in more detail.

Not in Our Image
In sorting through the subterranean expectations that influence how we behave, I tripped into something that strikes me as very important—but I had never really seen it before: our children get to screw up their lives in their own way. What I expect, not in my head but in my heart, is that all should be well, and I can help make that happen. I don't want to expect that all might not be well. and I can't do a darn thing. And I'm not sure I am able to believe, either, that all might be well, even if I am convinced it won't.

What I need to hold in my mind is the awareness that "I can't fix everything." While this goes, it seems, way beyond being a mother-in-law and also includes talking with my own ninety-three-year-old mother, as well as climatology, politics, and religion, it hits me the hardest in this mother-in-law stage. Sure, I should have learned this much earlier. I did not, and as I talk with other mothers, my slow learning is not so particular. We can love, support, counsel, and even assist. But we brought up our children to lead their own lives—and then, comes the time, we need to let them do it.

The year after our older son graduated from college, he was living in Chicago. He was starting a new business and working out of his cramped and cold apartment. I was in Houston, also working at home. Sometimes, in midafternoon, we would take a coffee and procrastination break together over the phone. One day I said to him, "I haven't seen you in ages. When are you coming home?" There was a very long pause, and then he said, "*I am* home." I felt like I had just been punched in the stomach. I was breathless for a moment while it hit me that his person hadn't simply gone to college. He had moved *out*. It wasn't very long after that that there was another woman in his house ... ummmm ... her house, their house.

Sometimes, getting our children through adolescence and, perhaps college, takes considerable effort. Many parents have sacrificed time, money, caring for themselves, even career options, to enable their children to have opportunities. Especially when the child-rearing years were stressful or demanding, we may think it should be easier when the children are grown. "I thought as I got older and my children became adults, they would help to take care of me," confides a single mother of two children who, in fact, are distracted by their own lives and careless of their mother's feelings. We want what we want. We have visions, hopes, wishes. And then, we get what we get. If, however, we focus on what we are not getting, and we make our unhappiness known, we run the risk of getting still less.

When mothers say, "All I want is for my child to be happy," I wish for them that this is true. ❧

CHAPTER THREE

From Ten Impossible Commandments To Seven Helpful Maxims

🐚

THE FINEST QUALITIES OF OUR NATURE, LIKE THE BLOOM ON FRUIT,
CAN BE PRESERVED ONLY BY THE MOST DELICATE HANDLING.

– Thoreau

There are, I have discovered, ten commandments for mothers-in-law. These rules are not mine. They come from mothers-in-law of every color, race, class, and disposition. Given the diversity of the women, the uniformity of opinion on this compels attention—also discussion.

Here are the ten most recommended rules:

1. Keep your mouth shut.
2. Keep your mouth shut.
3. Keep your mouth shut.
4. Keep your mouth shut.
5. Keep your mouth shut.
6. Keep your mouth shut.
7. Keep your mouth shut.
8. Keep your mouth shut.
9. Keep your mouth shut.
10. Keep your mouth shut.

If we all just followed the rules, this book could be one page long. We wouldn't need a book at all. With rules so simple, why is being a mother-in-law a challenge? Ah, we all know.

Even if we could follow the rule(s) and not say one word that would be heard as contentious, judgmental, argumentative, or critical—and more in a minute about why we so often cannot—our children would still hear contentions, judgments, arguments, and criticisms.

"You don't have to say anything Mom. We know what you are thinking," our children report. Often, they do. Just as we get the message when they roll an eye, curl a lip, shrug a shoulder, or agree in a tone of voice that indicates no agreement at all, they also know. But sometimes, they "know" when there is nothing to know. I can say, "Gee, it looks like rain," and my children hear, "She thinks I don't know how to dress or shut the windows, and why does she think I'm such a dunce?" What I meant, really, truly meant, was, "Gee, it looks like rain."

The problem is that there are, in truth, times when I have meant, "Do you really think it is a good idea to drive there just now?" or "Don't you want to take in the porch furniture?" or "I really don't want to talk about the weather but rather about this ridiculous course of action you are proposing?" Smart and intuitive as my fabulous sons are, they don't have perfect mother pitch. I confuse them. Sometimes, I confuse me.

And sometimes, our efforts to take care of one another, to keep our mouths shut, cause pain. One young woman told me that she agreed to spend a summer month with her in-laws in Maine. Her parents saw this as selfish and unfair. They didn't understand why, if she was willing to be away for a month, she couldn't spend two weeks with them—but they didn't actually say so. They just kind of sent annoyed signals. Of course, the daughter didn't say why she wanted to spend the month either because she was a bit embarrassed.

> It isn't that I love spending time with my in-laws more than my parents. But my in-laws have a big house just a few blocks from the beach. It is very hot in Dallas in the summer, and I appreciate being able to take the kids to the beach every day. My mother-in-law loves little children and enjoys playing with them, cooking meals, and being domestic. It is easy for me there. I adore spending time with my own parents, but they are less child centered. My father is distracted by the kids' noise. My mother is still working. It's less of a vacation for me when I'm there, and if I tell them this, they'll feel bad … and so will I.

In her mind, she had to say it all when, in fact, she could have just presented the reasons it made sense and let her parents figure out the whole story. But this is a considerate daughter. "I thought about it a lot, and now, we have concocted a plan to drive to Florida for a long weekend in March and meet my parents by the beach. Actually, we'll each have our own spaces. My husband can sail, the kids can play on the beach, my dad can read, and my mom and I can even shop. Perfect."

The roots of dissent can start with seemingly minor matters. Meet two lovely, family-oriented parents who are sane, sensible, and kind. Their oldest son is about to get married, and the mother is visibly upset because her about-to-be daughter-in-law insists on calling her Jane, when she so wants to be called "Mom." Jane has it in her mind that she is going to be mother to this young woman, and they will be close and intimate—and this is signified by the "Mom" title. The young woman feels she already has a mother; that title is taken. It makes perfect sense to the soon-to-be-bride—yet Jane feels rejected. Her disapproval is easily visible, and the young woman begins to worry that she is about to acquire a controlling, judging mother-in-law who had best be kept at a distance. Peevishness is taking root before anyone has cause to be peeved because each woman has a different take on what is "right."

Recently, I had an opinion about a long trip one of our sons and his wife planned to take. I wondered if it was the best idea, and if my daughter-in-law wasn't saying yes when she wanted to say no. When it came up in conversation, I didn't keep my mouth shut. I told my daughter-in-law my opinion ... really meaning to lend support if she wanted to say no. She reported to my son that I was deeply upset with their plans, and this upset my son. We had a tearful conversation in which I found myself explaining that there was just no way in the world I was going to be transformed into a woman without opinions. I would try to curb my impulses, but I have been spouting opinions for decades. Not likely I would become a paragon of "oh whatever" in the years ahead. I told my son that I found him to be smart and thoughtful. I thought he had good judgment, as did his wife. And, honestly, almost all of the time, I really didn't care all that much if they didn't agree with me. It was *just an opinion!*

So, if it is just an opinion and I'm not vested in the outcome, why do I need to put in my two cents? There is more to it than the pain of continual tongue biting. Talking, sharing ideas, opinions, plans, in my book, constitutes closeness. Of course, I also believe I know something, both about the world and about my kids, and hold on to the belief that my opinions are worth considering. I guess I still want to be a player in their lives. When our grown children decide my opinion is not right for them, it helps to hear why, and what is shaping their reasoning. Hearing their point of view somehow allows me to relax my hold on my own. Deborah Tannen has observed that, especially for women, exchanging details of daily life represents intimacy, but she explains the dangers:

The challenge in every relationship, every conversation, is to find ways to be as close as you want to be (and no closer) without that closeness becoming intrusive or threatening your freedom and your sense that you are in control of you life.

Tannen suggests that this is especially acute in relationships between daughters:

They combine, on one hand, the deepest connection, the most comforting closeness, with, on the other, the most daunting struggles for control. Each tends to overestimate the other's power while underestimating her own. And each yearns to be seen and accepted for who she is while seeing the other as who she wants her to be—or as someone falling short of who she should be.[1]

If my sons and daughters-in-law think I have no good ideas, no opinions worth hearing, no understanding of their lives—well, I feel depressed. That makes me feel older than any wrinkle. What kind of cream can I put on that? I see that my own mother needs to feel she is relevant in the world, and one way to feel that is to be relevant in my world. Telling me I need a better haircut or different shoes is as much about her need to be engaged with me as it is about my hair or shoes. It's hard to remember that because we are super sensitive to whatever our mothers say.

What about fathers? There are many fathers who feel called to give advice, and fathers-in-law are not exempt from being judged annoying, but isn't it interesting that fathers-in-law are not jokes? The feminine desire for connection shapes the nature of the conversation. Many fathers focus on factual matters ... who won the game, who's winning the election, how the plants are doing, what are the latest data on climate change. They avoid emotional issues, while mothers more often invite conversation about feelings, difficulties, and dreams. This generalization is supported by Tannen's research and by stories women tell about their own family relationships. There is something else that I think of as the "gender margin." Does it seem fathers/fathers-in-law are permitted a few degrees of "difficulty latitude" that women are denied? "I really don't know what my father-in-law thinks of me, now that you ask," a thoughtful thirty-three-year-old mother of two mused, "but I think quite a bit about what my mother-in-law thinks." Another young woman, thinking about her father and husband, comments, "Aren't men simpler than women? My dad is crotchety, but it's direct and uncomplicated."

I have been thinking about the kinds of interactions that come from a caring heart but seem to end with a cutting tongue. I notice that what makes me repetitive is not feeling heard—and what gets me in trouble is wanting to be heard. When I can't resist speaking up, and my kids are defensive before the sentences are fully formed, I seem to push harder, speak louder. I understand that this is not a good strategy. Once I feel truly heard and considered, I'm mostly willing to move on. I suspect they wish I didn't feel the need to be heard. What are we to do when we believe our children and/or their spouses can't/won't/don't hear us? Then again, what are they to do when they hear us, and we keep speaking anyway? What are they to do when they feel, feel deeply, that we are not hearing them?

We must follow the rule, bite our tongue, put a groove in it if needed. But there is more to this than just stuffing it. In my work now as an executive coach, I've learned that my job is not to teach my clients how to do this or that. The work is to uncover the assumptions, both conscious and unconscious, that inform their behaviors, especially those that keep them from being their most effective selves in the workplace. When I can be helpful to clients in developing new or expanded assumptions, assumptions the client decides make good sense and will be useful, then he or she will quickly figure out what to do to make it real. It can be awkward at first, and part of a coach's job is to help clients through the awkward stages. It is also the coach's job to help them stay focused on their new assumptions until those assumptions become hard-wired.

This mother-in-law business, I see, is not so different. I also have to give up some old assumptions—most especially the one about how incredibly wise and useful I am in my children's lives—and wire in some new thinking. With the help of lots of conversations with smart and experienced women, seven mother-in-law maxims have emerged to influence what comes out of my mouth. What I want is not to have to keep quiet on the outside while there is noisy, insistent conversation churning on the inside. There is just not much chance that in this state, the message, whether in words or in mood, will not seep out. The maxims that attract me are those that produce both inner and outer equanimity, that make me feel contented but not conflictual with my children and their partners.

Mother-in-Law Maxims:
1. She/He Who Runs the House, Sets the Rules.
2. Don't Get Attached to Outcomes.
3. Love Is Not a Competitive Sport.
4. Remember When You Were a Daughter-in-Law.
5. Speak Authentically and Kindly; Season with Humor.
6. Learning Happens Best from Experience.
7. Family Matters.

MAXIM 1: SHE/HE WHO RUNS THE HOUSE SETS THE RULES.

In our house, we decide. In the houses of our children, we follow. Maybe we believe the best way to load the dishwasher is left to right. Our daughter or daughter-in-law believes the right way to do it is back to front. In our house, the dishes should go in left to right, but we cannot try to make the point covertly and "teach" her the wisdom of our ways by putting the dishes in our way in her house. Furthermore, is this really important enough to wrangle around?

The person who runs the house gets to say how to do all those little things that make up a household. Of course, we will disagree. Mothers-in-law often want to just help by showing the young folk "the right way." We've got to give it up. The happiest mothers-in-law I've interviewed all have something to say about not getting hung up on the small stuff—and they do seem to think most of it is small.

Why do so many of us feel this huge pull to put in our two cents about housekeeping, fashion, child rearing, shopping, etc? Always, we want "to help" to save our children from their mistakes … but just what do we want to save them from—dirt, or excess labor, or misguidedness?

A bright and worldly book editor talked on the phone about how unsatisfying her relationships with her sons and their wives could be, and then she started talking about toilet training, a subject on which she had very firm opinions. Her children had not followed her advice. And their child was having some problems. Whether the problems were because they ignored the advice, or whether they ignored the advice because it didn't fit the child, there is no telling; but the result was that this issue had become a source of pain. I could hear that this woman really wanted to be helpful for her children—and I could also hear that it was not working. If we can come to understand that often the way to help, really help, is not to help, it would be less of a struggle to keep our mouths shut.

I see again and again that mothers want to keep from feeling irrelevant. We want to save ourselves from suspecting that the way we have always done things is not the only or the best or the most virtuous. After all, we have been the *important person* in a child's life for a long time, and it is a role we have come to cherish. When an outsider comes along to take over the role, it is a jolt to the system; the synapses, by habit, want to keep running the usual traps. When the outsider is not like us, we feel distance. Maybe we even feel a little wronged. If we can make the other more like us, well, won't we then be closer?

Once, when our boys were very little, we had to move from Bethesda, Maryland, to Chapel Hill, North Carolina. Both of our mothers came together for a weekend to allow us to go house hunting. We came back to find, to our satisfaction, both the children and the mothers in fine shape. I headed to the kitchen to make a celebratory dinner for us all. That kitchen had a long, large walk-in pantry with shelves where we kept both food and dishes. When I went into the pantry, I couldn't find anything. Everything was in a new place. I was horrified and went tearing into the living room asking what had happened. "Oh," my mother explained, "nothing was in the right place." It seemed that while my mother-in-law did what she enjoyed and played with the kids, my mother did what she enjoyed and rearranged my entire house. I was not grateful. And my mother was upset that I was not.

At the time, I was furious. How funny that I now understand the impulse when passing a daughter-in-law's closet. I could, I know, "help" her. Only a still-vivid memory of my own sense of indignation saves me from this entirely inappropriate impulse.

Because our children are emotionally attached to us, what we think so often matters hugely. Any hint that we don't think well of them hurts. We all have to keep working on knowing that, in adulthood, they are not us, and we are not them. Our quirks don't reflect in any way on their intelligence or good sense. In the same way, their idiosyncrasies are not about us. A happy mother-in-law, one who unabashedly declares, "I am a fabulous mother-in-law," has two sons and a daughter, all married with children and living nearby. "They all have very different ways of living and raising their children. I like some ways better than others, but my base belief is that it is their house, and they should do what they want in their house. Whether I think it is a good idea or not is not relevant."

A woman I know responded to her teenager's complaints about

her parenting by telling him, "Honey, here is the good news: If I am not a perfect parent, you don't have to be a perfect kid." In adulthood, if our children don't lead perfect lives and please us with every behavior, well then, we are allowed to be imperfect too.

MAXIM 2: DON'T GET ATTACHED TO OUTCOMES

An *intention* is something we hope to accomplish. The *process* is how we go about getting from this intention to an outcome, and the *outcome* is what, in the end, actually happens.

It isn't at all difficult to understand this sequence. The tricky part is to set the right intention. If my intention is to find a perfect red straw hat with a blue band and fat peonies, I could find myself very disappointed. If my intention is to look fabulous for a spring fête by finding a great hat, the odds of success go up. If my intention is to find a way to have a lovely afternoon, I have still more options. So maybe I set my intention to look great. The process I choose might be hat shopping and, more specifically, shopping with my friend Nancy. The outcome ... well, how about if I leave that open, and we'll see what happens. I might end up with a fabulous new green dress and wear last year's hat with complete contentment if I can let go of that red hat thing.

We get in trouble when we confuse intention and outcome. Getting fixated on just how things should be is a setup for disappointment. For example, one mother always imagines how she, her daughter, and her daughter-in-law will go shopping together, and she has a perfect picture in her mind of how it will be. She is always disappointed because the event never follows her script. Her intention is to have a good time with her girls, but she is so clear about what constitutes a good time that when something else happens, she feels let down.

When we decide something will make our children's lives nicer or easier, and then they are not so appreciative, we get hurt. Often, isn't it because we decide, in advance, without input, on what action would make them happy, and then we get locked on the action ... and forget our intention was to make them happy? "My wonderful, generous in-laws want to take us to great restaurants and buy us good wines every time they visit. But most of the time they are here, it is a work night, and I'm too tired to go out and not up for wine. I would be thrilled if we opened a can of tomato soup and made grilled cheese sandwiches, but I don't have the heart to tell them that the dinners that are fun for them are work for us."

From what I'm hearing, one common fixation has to do with cleanliness. Cleanliness, of course, is a fine thing. Clean houses are surely better than dirty houses. But that is a trick pronouncement because it does not mean that cleaning houses is better than not cleaning them. There must be a whole subset of women who feel that "that other woman"—and it can be the mother or mother-in-law as well as daughter or daughter-in-law—keeps a disgraceful house and needs to get with the virtues of cleanliness.

But it is much easier, much, much easier to have a clean house if you don't mind cleaning or, even if you mind, it is a habit to which you have allowed yourself to become accustomed. What if you dislike housekeeping and prefer to play with the kids, paint, read, get a Ph.D., or work on your tennis game? What if you are working full time in a demanding job, and there really isn't time or money for higher standards? What if you don't care so much that you live in disorder? Don't a few germs actually build up the kids' immune systems?

So be it. She who likes to clean may clean, and she who does not, or finds she cannot, need not. As to the complaint that "my son didn't grow up in a house like this," he clearly has adjusted. If he wants a cleaner house, it is his fight, not yours.

The point of this discussion is not really cleanliness, but how difficult it is to expect people to do things they don't like to do and/or don't value. What is easy for us may not be easy at all for someone else. We don't get to tell them that, really, it isn't so hard at all. We don't get to show them unless we are asked to do so. We don't get to insist on the importance of an outcome we cherish in order to make them follow a process that isn't comfortable.

It took fourteen years before one daughter-in-law explained to her mother-in-law, a woman who saw herself as "enormously helpful when I visit," what she really felt: "When you offer to clean up, or start actually doing it, you make me feel like a failure."

"But isn't cleaning up the living room for guests a sign of respect and affection?" the mother of this messy daughter-in-law and her messier son groans. The children think inviting her and wanting her to step into their lives is what signals affection. Our children and their spouses may not like to do the things we like, share our values, see our perspectives. In fact, given the attraction of opposites, there may be little overlap. While I really want to believe that it is a daughter or son-in-law's job to make nice and win us over, in fact, unfortunately, it works the other way round. We have to try to love the person the child we love marries. We can *intend* to win him or her over, and that means focusing on the process of building a relationship, not on any specific habit.

My friend George told me he decided that he chose each of his children's spouses. At first, I thought he was telling me he had arranged their marriages, but, no, they had followed their hearts, and once they decided to marry, he told himself this was, in fact, the very person he wished to have as a son- or daughter-in-law and set about doing all he could to make it true. Sort of like some advice I once heard a therapist offer: "Fake it 'til you make it."

While it might be nice sometimes if we could control others, the bottom line is we are the only ones we control. If it is someone else's job, we really have no control over the situation. I am learning that it is easy to avoid getting hurt and giving hurt when I hold to the intention of being seen as loving, and I think about what processes might help me. I do get attached to outcomes, but knowing the dangers helps me step away and go back to that "be loving" mantra.

MAXIM 3: LOVE IS NOT A COMPETITIVE SPORT

"Why does he always get to sit in the front seat ...? His half of the cookie is bigger than mine ...! You let her do that so why can't I ...?" Those plaintive wails from our children's growing years are, but for the grandkids, seemingly behind us. But it seems many of us are not yet done with competition.

In many conversations with mothers, competition appears in many permutations. Earlier, I wrote about the woman whose son-in-law felt competitive with her. Sometimes it is we who feel competitive with our children's spouses. We wish for more time and attention. We wish a spouse's needs didn't always trump ours. We think a son- or daughter-in-law doesn't really understand what is going on with our child. We worry. It is the rare woman who can completely stop worrying about her children.

So worry if you must—but you cannot compete with your child's spouse. Remember this: there is no possible win. If you win, you have been a lousy mother. If you lose, it hurts like hell. Your child has got to choose to have and hold, honor and cherish the spouse. That is what it means to have a good marriage. Isn't part of parenting helping our kids get ready for the next steps in their lives? Daughters-in-law and sons-in-law can never be our competitors, and we, as mothers-in-law, cannot compete with them for our child's time or money or affection. We need our own lives.

We know that in order to hold on, we have to let go. Our kids taught us this when they were teenagers. In order to be loving, I remind myself, I have to let them love others. In order to have them ask for advice, I have to keep silent until asked. And I have to know that if love is elastic, time is not. What it may mean is that our child doesn't have as much time for us—and damn it anyway. But establishing a life, a career, a family, a household, a social structure takes tons of time, and that doesn't always leave much time for the people you already know who are supposed to love you no matter what. As I watch our younger son, on the cusp of thirty-four, I see him juggling a new and growing business, a house, a new baby, a wife, a desire to exercise and have some friends, and, as well, a need to stay in touch with family. It is a lot, and there are weeks when I call or text message, and he just doesn't have the time to respond. This is not about me. This is about him and all he is juggling.

One of my daughters-in-law is in the midst of job hunting. I am eager for every detail—and I get very few. It is not because she wants to keep me at a distance, but because she does not feel the need to share. She has complicated feelings about this job struggle, and talking about it is not relaxing but stressful. She is taking care of herself, and it sometimes happens that this is different from taking care of me. Oh, I guess it is *my* job to take care of me. Well, drat ...

There are three other kinds of competition that women mentioned. One is the competition between mothers—his and hers. "Mothers can give advice that mothers-in-law can't touch. I am the mother of sons, and my daughters-in-law are close to their mothers. I sometimes feel left out. The wives set the agendas, and my good sons follow their lead, and I'm hanging out wishing for something different."

Mothers and daughters seem more likely to go shopping, lunching, or beautifying together. Some mothers, who live in the same town as their sons, have workday lunch dates with their sons. Some spoke of having time together, sharing hobbies like hiking or analyzing stocks. Some orchestrate mother-son babysitting on weekends. Still, many mothers wish it were as easy to find one-on-one time with men as with women.

In a different kind of in-law competition, one mother felt "replaced" by her daughter's mother-in-law. "I am outgoing, demanding, pro-fessional, and competitive. This woman is quiet, complacent, undemanding, really quite lovely, but completely unlike me. My daughter is so drawn to her that I experience it as a repudiation of my mothering, of me. It creates a still greater distance between me and my daughter."

A second competition is between the different sets of parents.

One set of parents in the Southeast was thrilled when their son, living in the West, chose a girl from this hometown. "Ah, we'll get to see more of them this way, and maybe they will even move back here, we thought. Now, when they come, they are always at her parents' house, and it is disappointing. But worse, her father lets us know that he is paying for this or that, sending a check, or picking up an expense. We can't always do it. We don't want to do it, and yet we feel, what?...'lesser?' for being less generous."

No way this boy's family can say to this girl's family, "Hey, don't give them so much." Perhaps they can speak with their son, and let him know that they are pleased for his good fortune and won't be matching the gifts, and hope it will not cause a differential in family relationships. When one half of a couple comes from lots, and the other comes from less, or comes with a different view of how to use their money, both sides ought to ramp up their awareness. The give-lots side ought to be careful of the feelings of others and remember that giving money is not the only important gift. The give-less side has got to manage their emotions, so they don't pop out around other issues that are unrelated and recognize that they have gifts to give that are not material. "The other in-laws have lots of money," said a college professor, and, in our view, they spoil our grandchildren with extravagant gifts and trips. We are at a disadvantage, and we don't think it is so good for the kids, but their parents permit it, and there is nothing we can do but try to build as solid a relationship with our grandchildren as we can at the emotional rather than the materialistic level."

The in-laws of one of my college roommates did a nice thing. She came from a solidly middle class family, comfortable but not wealthy. She married money. Shortly before the wedding, her about-to-be father-in-law took her aside and handed her a large check, saying, "My wife and I believe that every woman should have money of her own. This is not a gift for both of you. This is just for you, and we hope you will open your own account and know that you have access to funds that are yours alone." A woman with no ability to give money but a wicked talent on the sewing machine offered to monogram her new daughter-in-law's initials on lingerie and towels. We give what we have to give, and what matters most is the love we give.

Let's go back to the immigrant analogy again. What if we regard the other in-laws as, well, odd? A daughter-in-law's Chinese mother found all the family kissing at her daughter's wedding quite strange. His parents were perplexed by the need to change dresses three times at the rehearsal dinner. So one's family's normal is another's weird, and vice versa, and can we see it as a gift? If our grandchildren learn customs that are strange to us, won't it only make them more adaptable, flexible adults? And if we learn along the way, just maybe we'll get a bit more flexible too. Can't hurt.

The competition, of course, comes when their normal interferes with our normal. "We always go to church Christmas Eve," one mother explains. "My daughter's in-laws always give out gifts on Christmas Eve. We want the kids with us, and they want the kids with them, and someone always feels bad." And probably the people feeling the worst are the adult children caught between their parents. "We ate three Thanksgiving meals last year," a thirty-four-year-old husband and father reports. We did my family at noon, her family at five, and we arrived just in time for the dessert with our good friends on the street. If I keep that up, I'll never make forty."

If we frame differing needs as a competition, somebody has to lose. If we see it as the inevitable result of bringing more people, more needs, more traditions to the table, it may help us recognize that, sometimes, it just makes good sense to change things a bit for the sake of harmony and happiness. So, start going to church Christmas morning, or give your children the gift of not feeling pressure to be with you when you want to go. We naturally think getting our way is winning, but sometimes, letting someone else win turns out to be a win for us as well.

The last competition is among children. One daughter or daughter-in-law feels another is favored, one son is more accepted than another, one grandchild seems to be more loved than another.

Believe me, the younger generation is highly sensitized to this—and we might not even be aware of their feelings. If any of our children or their spouses brings toxic relationships to the dinner table, how must we react? Do we protect that child? Do we shame him or her? Do we beg the adult siblings to make nice?

When our sons were little, we could tell them they had to share, they couldn't hit, and they had to play together. We can't tell that to adult children. The recommendation that sounds right to me is the Texas big mama who says, "My days of mediating are over, Sugar. It's up to my children to work out their own relationships, and if they can't all sit at my table together, then they need to tell me what they want me to do, and I'll usually do it. I am here for all my kids ... but not necessarily at the same time."

Children are competitive with each other, even when they have children of their own. "Because my sister lives near my mother, it is so easy for them to go shopping together, and my mom buys her clothes that she never buys for me," complains one adult daughter who feels, against her better judgment, put out. A mother talks about the different economic circumstances of her three daughters. One is married to a sweet and loving husband whose career and financial prospects are rocky. One is married to a successful businessman who the parents think is controlling and limiting their accomplished daughter's life, and the third is married to a man who works in the family business and is drawn into the family orbit.

> My daughters and I are all very close, and my opinions about their spouses are a challenge. What I do, and I have had to learn this, is never discuss one of their spouses with their sisters, never make comments about any of the husbands to any of the girls. I do try to encourage each daughter to be the very best person she can be and to know I love and admire her. I just don't comment on their marriages, and on the rare occasions that they need to ventilate, I listen and bite my tongue.

There are three basic strategies to help us ameliorate competitive tensions. First, never, not ever, compare one child or child's spouse with another. Remember how we learned that we were not to compare our children ... no, "... but Peter gets good grades; why can't you ..." Of course, we mustn't chide one child to act like another, but we also must be careful singing praises. You think you are simply saying what a great mother one young woman is, but another who is not spotlighted hears implied criticism.

Second, rewards and benefits should be distributed equally unless circumstances demand the equal treatment might, in fact, be unfair treatment. A mother I know has three adult children. Her two sons are highly successful professionals. Her daughter, who does not have salaried work, is married to a man who earns significantly less than his brothers-in-law. The mother has paid for some educational expenses for her daughter's children, but before she did so, she sat down with each of her sons and had a frank and open conversation with them about what she wanted to do and why. She told them that with this gift, she could assure equality of education for all the grandchildren. The sons agreed, and there is, for this family, no acrimony.

A final tactic is state of mind. We can decide that for our generation it is okay to be runner up, so long as the runner up gets a medal too. One mother takes care of the grandbabies three times a week. The other mother babysits once a month. Yes, there will be a different relationship. So be it. By the time our children are old enough to marry, we surely have learned that all is not "fair." Sometimes, we don't get the "fair share" for which we hoped. A sure way to guarantee less is to whine, so don't do it. It is less important, I am thinking, to get the most love so long as we get enough.

MAXIM 4: REMEMBER WHEN YOU WERE A DAUGHTER-IN-LAW

It is easy to be disappointed if our daughters-in-law or our daughters are too busy to spend time with us. We forget that we were often too busy for our own mothers-in-law. Now, looking back, I am sorry I was not a better daughter-in-law. I preferred that the parents come to us rather than we to them. It seemed so much easier for them to travel than for our circus to take to the road. I expected them to adjust to our schedule, our needs, our desires. So why do I sometimes find myself thinking my grown children should really be adjusting to us? It would work much better for us to see them in the middle of July, but they prefer Labor Day. We like dinner at seven, but they prefer eight or eight-thirty. All adults negotiate around such preferences, so why does it sometimes feel more personal with children?

This process of remembering our own feelings can have funny results. One woman talked about how her own fond memories didn't lead to right action.

> My mother did something I thought was wonderful. When we came to visit, she always insisted on paying for the plane tickets. Her point of view was that she didn't want us not visiting because money was tight. It was a gift to her to have us visit, and she wanted to make it easy. Fortunately, we can afford to be equally generous and want to pass this huge kindness on. Yet, I sometimes think my newest daughter-in-law sees it as suggesting my son is not able to provide well, or that we want them to be beholden; there is something that gives me the unarticulated message that this is a bad idea.

So, just as we can't do to others what we hated having done to us, similarly, just because some kindness worked wonderfully for me doesn't mean it is a good idea to pass on. Gotta read the clues, pick up on the signals, and not be righteous about how great I am. Okay, that last bit is asking a lot, I know. I think I would have loved having a mother-in-law like me. I do think I'm kinda wonderful and am more than willing to make my daughters-in-law's lives as nice as I can. But what I think makes them nice is not always what they think makes them nice. The golden rule says do unto others as you would have done unto you. The mother-in-law rule says do unto others as they would have done unto them.

A young woman who lives with her husband and two very charming children in the middle of Manhattan admires her mother-in-law and appreciates the many kindnesses she offers, but how much she wishes her mother-in-law did not want to spend her entire visit working out and getting spa treatments.

> I know she thinks I ought to be more fit and would love to have me come to the gym with her, but I just don't feel comfortable there. What I would really like is for us to have tea together and just chat about what is going on in our lives. I wish I knew how to make that happen. I do invite her, but she is off to some appointment, and I can't seem to capture her attention.

So often, when in-laws come to visit, and the husband goes off to work, the wife finds herself home for ten hours with her in-laws. I have trouble spending ten straight hours with a dear old friend, let alone people I acquired in a marriage. If you loved spending time with your own mother-in-law, it might be hard to find it doesn't work the same with a daughter-in-law. If you didn't like spending so much time with a mother-in-law, then you should understand perfectly how it goes. Were you a working mother who could barely keep it all together without visitors and found yourself feeling like you were drowning when in-laws came to visit? This requires straight talk: "What would you like?" we can ask, wanting an honest answer. "How long do you think we should visit? Can I be helpful around the house, or do you need a few hours alone each day?"

We don't see ourselves as the spouses of our children see us. What our own children find familiar, someone else can find threatening, discourteous, confusing. If we have judgments about those people our children married, it makes sense that they might have a few judgments about us. And if they are off base, could we also be off base? If we realize, after many years of marriage, that we did not see our own mothers-in-law in all their dimensions, it makes sense that the people our children marry may not see us fully—and we may not see them fully. We are so aware of what we are doing to make things work without mentioning our efforts. I believe our children and their spouses feel the same way ... that we often fail to appreciate all they are doing to make things work as we, perhaps, thought our own in-laws didn't grasp our efforts.

One of the greatest—and sometimes hardest—gifts we can offer our children and their spouses is to stop judging them. Letting go of judging means more than not talking about our judgments. It means not thinking them either. We can just let go of whatever we wish they would do, be, say and accept them in our minds as they are. We can go further and look for things they do that make sense for them and for their family and, again, without comment, focus on the good. Even when we always keep quiet, that judging function vibrates in the air and can be felt. Loving, however, also vibrates and can be felt.

MAXIM 5: SPEAK AUTHENTICALLY; SPEAK KINDLY; SEASON WITH HUMOR

The fourth maxim leads to this fifth, and maybe this is the most challenging. Part of good relations, loving relations, means being able to speak honestly and truthfully. My family will tell you, with a hint of resignation, that I am called to speak from what seems to me to be a deeply honest place. It has taken some time for me to learn that, authentic as I may feel, I should not say whatever is on my mind, whenever I feel the need to say it. Yes, speaking from the heart is a good thing, but it is a better thing when I speak in such a way that what I say will be well received. Sometimes, it is probably best that, actually, I don't speak at all.

Beginning a thought about a child's spouse with "*She* or *He*" is a nonstarter—unless some delicious, uncomplicated compliment is going to follow. If we think what we are about to say will hurt, we have got to stop and find another way of approaching the issue. I can't write that a parent's job is always to accept whatever is presented. I want real relationships, not phony, make-believe nice. But always letting our children know when our feelings are hurt usually does not make them want to spend more time with us.

We need to set our minds to send signals to the body so the body will just know what to do. You know, it's how we drive. The brain notes "left turn," and away the car goes without conscious thought on our part. If we envision kindness, if we hold to the intention that, without giving up any part of our true selves, we can be and want to be kind to our children and their partners, then I think we stand a better chance of having our bodies act in kindly ways. Does that mean we won't ever screw up? Nah ... but we'll run a better score.

Apologizing is an act of kindness, not wimpiness. Okay, here is one of my most embarrassing and demeaning moments. I was out to lunch with my mother. We were at very nice restaurant. Two minutes into the lunch, my mother told me something that bothered her. I don't even remember the substance, but I indicated that I heard her, but the subject was not going to be on the table that day and to please let it go. Five minutes later, she was back on point. And before the main course, during the main course and over coffee, she kept kicking this dead horse. Finally, I said, "Mom, if you raise this again, I'm going to hit you." So, when we were walking to the car and she did it again, well, I sort of gave her a punch in the arm. No, I didn't hit hard, but I, a forty-something adult, am hitting my sixty-something mother in the parking lot. *What* was I thinking?

As I replay this embarrassing episode in my mind, I feel, all over again, that her behavior was inappropriate. But mine was more inappropriate. My regret, then and now, is not my unwillingness to comply with her wishes but my inability to maintain my composure. Whether or not she was sorry for the provocation didn't matter. I am in charge of me, and I have to be responsible for my actions. That means I do not get to demean my mother, even when she insists on pushing my buttons repeatedly. I don't get to do it because, first, I really don't want to hurt or embarrass my mother, and second, I don't want to be the kind of person who acts with such a total lack of composure.

My husband has a rare and lovely ability to use humor to deflect provocation. When my mother gets going, he charms her, he teases her, he deflects her. He finds a bit of humor or whimsy in the conversation and shifts the emphasis. He was less successful doing this with his own mother, but after watching him for a couple decades with mine, I have finally gotten the point. My mother lets me know that she doesn't think it is a good idea that I buy a new car. I can respond with facts, with logic, with the repair record of the current car, or, better, I can say, well if I'm going to do a dumb thing, should I really go for broke and consider a Bentley or maybe an antique roadster? "How about a yellow Porsche convertible? You know, Mom, we could buy it together, and I would let you drive it."

When I do want to be clear about my feelings, I am learning simply to say what I mean and not try to couch it in some clever verbal fortune cookie. I am learning this because my children see right through my subterfuges. If I know them, they know me. But I am also learning to figure out what I really mean. I do it by trying out the message on good friends or my husband. I get the whining out of my system, and they tell me when I sound accusatory or unreasonable. As I talk through what I am feeling, I get clearer about what is causing the feelings and clearer about how to speak so that I can be well received.

You know, it slows you down, this careful consideration. It's like cautious driving. It may take longer to get there, but you are much less likely to crash and burn. When I want to scratch at my children about something, I know I have to ask what is it that I want that I'm not getting. Think about that urge to clean a daughter-in-law's closet. When I ask myself why I care ... what I would get if the closet were neater ... I can't figure out a single gain for me. If the answer is nothing, what's the big deal?

A daughter-in-law I met at a business meeting heard the topic of my book and immediately began telling me about how her mother-in-law sends oblique messages about how wrong it is to work professionally while the children are still little. Her mother-in-law, she understands, does this because she believes it will be better for the children, and there is time to work later. But it doesn't come out that way. "Look," the daughter-in-law says. "I know what she is thinking. I have read all the studies. My husband and I have discussed this. We have talked about every friend we had when we were little and tried to remember if they had working mothers or not. I don't want to stay home all day. I want to work, and my husband wants me to work. She needs to stop it because it is none of her business." In this instance, to get the tension out in the open, it might be helpful for the mother-in-law to speak about her fears for her grandchildren to both the son and his wife, but also for this mother/mother-in-law to promise to work on trusting them to be good parents.

My parents always stayed in a hotel when they visited us. We liked it. It gave us a little space at the end of the day. Now I am the visiting grandparent, and my children seemed surprised that we prefer paying to stay at the local bed and breakfast to their newly renovated guest room. I found myself starting to weave a story about how it was better for them if we stayed in the B&B. And then I stopped.

"Look, I know it's nice to have family just wander down to breakfast in a robe in the morning, and I love that you want us to stay here. But we are odd souls, and we just like having our own space." Speaking the truth didn't mean they thought we were sensible people, but I think they understand. All young people will not feel comfortable, in turn, speaking from their hearts to their mothers-in-law, but if we can model speaking authentically and can report our needs without signaling that we want a certain answer, we up the odds of getting the full scoop.

As I was sitting at the computer editing this very section, a good friend from graduate school called as if she had been reading my mind. We began chatting about travel and friends and books, but then she shared a story with me that clearly was meant to go on the page.

> My daughter-in-law and I have never really had a great relationship. It's always been polite, and on the surface we did fine, but I never felt she really was at ease with me. I think she felt I judged her, and the truth is, when I think about it, I did judge her. My judging wasn't helped the time I discovered I was the only grandparent without a picture in the baby book. There were a few more incidents that increased my discomfort so much that I decided I simply had to say something.
>
> But I could never figure out what to say that would not make things worse. I kept trying this out on friends and looking for the right words and couldn't find them. Finally, I decided I was going to have to live with this situation and make it as good as I could. It came to me then how much I wanted my mother and mother-in-law to think I was a great person and how hard I tried to please them in ways that were subtle but important to me. So, instead of being my usual confrontational self, I just starting trying as hard as I could to be nice, to judge less. I have been this young woman's mother-in-law for over ten years. Now, in just these last months, my daughter-in-law is warmer and more open to me than ever. Isn't that amazing?

MAXIM 6: LEARNING HAPPENS BEST FROM EXPERIENCE

You know how little girls can be four going on forty. I was like that. I was a very mature little girl at ten, so it is no surprise that at thirty-three, with two babies, a 2,200-square-foot house, a part-time job and, finally, my own washer and dryer, I felt exceptionally grown-up. We had already moved several times, and I was juggling house, husband, kids, work, money, and friends quite well, thank you. I understood a lot. I had excellent powers of analysis. I was compassionate, thoughtful, and reflective. Wasn't I terrific!

I don't know how terrific I was then, but I know for sure that however much I knew then, I know more now. I am more compassionate, thoughtful, and reflective. I manage situations differently and, I think, more effectively. I did lots of things right in those years, but I also made lots of mistakes. I have not learned from them all—there were too many—but I have learned.

One thing I have learned is that I learn best from experience. Lectures, books, audiotapes, friends' advice are no substitute for jumping off the cliff myself. I could have saved myself a lot of hard landings if I could have learned more from the experiences of others. And sometimes I did. But often, I learned by doing— doing well and doing not so well. So, isn't the next generation going to need experience? Thinking about this does help with an attitude shift. Instead of believing that I can save my kids from what I construe as mistakes, trouble, screw ups, I am cultivating a different point of view. It isn't the mind-my-own-business model that some recommend. There is no way I can embrace an assumption that my children's lives are not my business at all. I just care too much. But I think I can move toward a marketing model ... put the information out there in the market-place, with all the other competing bits of information, and let the buyer sort and sift. And if my product is rejected, it's not personal, not the product or the person. It's just what happens. I had the chance to make my own choices. My sons and their spouses deserve the chance to make theirs.

I laughed my way through a conversation with a funny woman who explained how she knew instantly that the man her daughter brought home was entirely unacceptable. He was, she decided, arrogant, rude, and self-absorbed. It was only when forced to make a two-hour drive together, just the two of them, that she discovered they shared a sense of what was funny. They talked to each other easily and had lots in common. It was in the car that she saw all the good qualities her daughter recognized and realized she had not given this young man, now her beloved son-in-law of four years, a chance.

Our children have had experiences we have not had. Their world is not the same. Many students I worked with when I taught leadership-capacity building would come to my office to say, for example, that they had to be premeds because their parents insisted, even though they wanted to major in art history. Often, these were the children of immigrants who were determined that their kids would have the American dream. They gave their children their very best advice, but sometimes they gave it in the context of their own lives and not the lives of their children. I never suggested these students not listen to their parents. I did not love them as much as their parents, and I was not going to stick with them forever. We did talk about contexts and options, about assumptions and values, and how decisions did not have to be made for all time at age twenty. We talked about whether it was possible to keep options open and to appreciate how much their parents cared for and worried about them.

If I want my children to listen to me, I have to listen to them, yes, really listen. I have to understand their frameworks, their assumptions. Sometimes, I am guilty of not being an A+ listener. I want to interpret, insert, intrude into their story. When I step outside myself and watch what happens when I do that, I see that it shuts down the conversation. Their agenda is not the same as my agenda, and why should it be? Our job is not to fix their "misguided" agendas but to respect them and allow them to set their own course.

The biggest new assumption I have had to embrace is that my

job is no longer to raise children, to guide them, keep them from harm, teach them. What they want from me is love, applause, approval, affection. It's hard to appreciate that I am just reaching the fullness of my maturity, beginning to get wise as well as smart, and now my main role is to stand on the sidelines and be the cheerleader. But, HooRay, go team. What the hell, cheerleaders seem to look good.

MAXIM 7: FAMILY MATTERS

My children don't need to get along with me or my husband to have satisfactory lives. Plenty of families behave like foreign nations. I probably need them more, but, yes, survival is possible if my daughters-in-law don't warm to my charms and keep me at some distance.

But it is so much better when we can have a supportive and loving family. When there are grandchildren, they are enriched by having grandparents they know and love and who are clearly head-over-heels crazy over the grandkids. Adult children are helped when they have parents or in-laws who can give support, love, and assistance. It's more fun to be part of a loving family than a tense one.

I take this to mean that my job, at the most basic level, is the same as it always was: to be loving and nurturing and make the family work. What I have to do for that to work is, however, different from what I had to do when my boys were living in the upstairs bedrooms. Of course, it isn't only *my* job. I am married, and there are two of us in the parent category, two of us in the in-law category, but the mother's role is different than the father's, and *mother-in-law* evokes its own reactions. In interview after interview, it is most often the mother who seems to feel the tensions of family life most acutely. One young woman wondered if it wasn't because the mothers-in-law caused most of the tension. A central exploration of this book, of course, is how and why tensions occur.

Mainly, I must focus on what my job is because it is the only one over which I have control. I hope my children feel they also have some responsibility for family connectivity, but I can't make them do as

I wish. I was told I needed to hear the story of a woman in the Midwest with "a horrible in-law situation." This woman was divorced when her only child was young, and she raised him alone. They had a close and pleasurable relationship and sometimes traveled together as adults. Around thirty, he met and married a lawyer who came from a large family. His mother never warmed to this woman, and it seems she did not warm toward her mother-in-law. The couple had three children, and since they both maintain demanding work lives, the woman's parents moved into the young couple's house. The "other mother" feels excluded. She has a list of complaints about her daughter-in-law, including the demeaning and argumentative way she speaks to her husband. She spoke of being bewildered about why her relationship with her son has deteriorated to barely speaking. It's very hard when our children marry people we don't like very much, and, perhaps, they don't like us. It spoils things. It dampens our hopes. It can change our lives. It feels unfair. It is.

But it is interesting in the story above that all the blame focuses on the wife. What responsibility do our own children have in making family work? If a daughter- or son-in-law speaks to us in demeaning ways in front of our own children, shouldn't we first think about why our children acquiesce? If the price of peace in one family is disharmony in another, do we want that? If an adult child finds himself or herself with a difficult partner and decides to make it work, can we complain about the strategies they use to keep the peace?

There is very little that can happen that is worth getting in the way of having a loving family. I believe that with my all my head and heart. The problem, at least for me, is not in understanding the unimportance of most stuff but giving up its grip on me. The only thing that seems to work is to remind myself that the satisfaction of being right is not worth losing the affection of my sons. If I incur the wrath of my daughters-in-law, my sons must side with their wives. The same has to be true for daughters. If we want them to love the people with whom they live, it helps if we can love them too. Remember the song lyrics, "Ain't Nobody Happy If Momma Ain't Happy?" I ain't the momma they are talking about any more.

I was reminded of the importance parents may continue to play in their children's lives by a young woman I adore. Because we are not family, it seems easier to share our feelings. One day, she gave me something she had written in her journal, writing provoked by conversations about this book. In reading her thoughts, you should know that I consider this woman grounded, mature, happy in her life. She is a contented wife and mother who has parents she loves and admires, so do not read her private thoughts and think this is a needy person. It is not true.

> Honest thought from my heart—how to get closer to me: I still want my parents to *notice* me ... *more*. They seem distracted by ten million other things. They should ponder and notice how wonderful I am. Probably, they notice, but it feels that they don't show it. And I hate it when I tell them about a decision I have made, and they tell me it's the *right* one. *Ohhhh*, that irks me. It's like I passed the invisible test that is always there, but I can't see the questions or the benchmarks. It suggests to me that when I share something, and they say, "interesting," or zone out, that I made a wrong choice and didn't pass. I end up feeling like I didn't make the decision that makes them feel good. Whenever I have a sitter come, it is "good"; when I entertain the idea of work, it is "good"; ... there is never a conversation opened up about my thoughts and what I am weighing.

> Okay, so what's the reciprocal for my parents? What do I do to them too often?

Wow. I read this and thought, oh my, this isn't simple. I'll bet my own children harbor similar thoughts. Do they feel I am judging? Am I judging? Do I grasp, in spite of all the words I've written about loving so far, how much they still need to feel part of the family and to be loved and praised? And do her parents fear to say anything, as I sometimes do, because they will push buttons? Do they not open a conversation about, say work, because they know they have different views than their daughter and the conversation will be too charged from the start?

Some of you will read this and think, "Oh for heaven's sake. All of you need to grow up and get on with your lives and quit worrying so much." That's not a bad philosophy ... when it works. But if you are getting on, and your child is wishing for more, or your grown child is feeling very self sufficient, and you feel shut out, that yearning for a closer family can become a chronic ache. Every pain is important to the person who is feeling it, and when it is our children who ache, we tend to feel it as well.

These seven maxims do not promise perfect equanimity. Ah, if only! They won't transform people we regard as difficult into charmers. They won't guarantee sweetness and light at every encounter. What they do for me is help me to understand what my role should be, what part I have to play in the family drama, in this deep desire that if I get it right, it will help others to get it right. If I hold to the belief that we can and should find ways to enjoy and engage one another, and I walk, as much as I can, in that direction all the time, my presence will have power.

And when I get it wrong, I am going to remember the quote I love at the start of chapter 8: "Nothing is a big deal. It's whatever it is, and then it's something else."

CHAPTER FOUR

Looking Down From the Balcony

❦

IT IS NORMAL TO HAVE LARGE GAPS BETWEEN OUR VALUES AND OUR
BEHAVIORS. IT IS ALSO NORMAL TO DENY THAT THESE GAPS EXIST.

– Robert E. Quinn in *Change the World*

It would be wonderful if every now and then, like in movies
about angels or ghosts who become humans, we could
divide in two, leave one version of ourselves in place, and
take a duplicate up several levels to look down and watch the
family dynamics at play from a distance. I know we would be
surprised at what would be revealed because it's so easy to see what

is going on in other families with great clarity—and they can't see it at all. We get stuck in familiar patterns, and we keep repeating them … and keep getting irritated at the results.

This is a little example, but all those little things accumulate into something bigger. I love my older son's hair when it is a bit longer and gets soft and curly. He likes it short and straight. Whenever I see him with his hair longer, out of my mouth comes, "Oh, I love your hair curly like that. It's so becoming." And every time he says, "Yeah, I need a haircut. It's too long for me." What he is hearing with his inner ear is probably something like, "Why does she always have to say that! She says what she likes as if because she likes it, it is better. She wants to tell me how to do everything. I get to run my own life, and when is she going to get it?"

Why do I do this? I do not want to be critical, judgmental, and meddling. I just wish, you know, he would wear his hair longer. I've spent some time thinking about how to explain this and talking with my psychologist friends. It took mulling and a large portion of humble pie to bring the answer into focus. I think I do it because I believe, deep down, that what I think is right, and since I'm his mother, hardwired to give him directions, it's okay to tell him and, really, because I love him so much, know him so well, and have such good judgment, he should listen. It isn't really an answer that makes one feel proud, is it?

Yes, I am his mother. And, at this stage, it doesn't matter how he wears his hair. There is no "right." He needn't obey, and I have got to change that wiring that allows me trip these synapses so quickly. What I see from the balcony is that the issue is not hair. It is my difficulty in evolving my parental role. I only thought it was about hair.

Daniel Siegel is a developmental psychiatrist who studies and writes about parent-child attachment in the early years. Siegel says that our expectations, perceptions, and behavior interact with our child's inborn temperament and in that intersection of two person-alities, the parent-child transaction is shaped. Furthermore, how we behave with our children is directly affected by the attachment history we have with our own parents.[1]

In short, what happened to us influences what happens to our kids. The very early years set in motion a pattern of interacting for the future. What if the pattern Siegel is describing gets repeated yet again in our early bonding with a son- or daughter-in-law? What if the way we attach at the start of the relationship influences what happens next? And what if, in fact, the same unconditional love strategy that is required at birth for the healthiest of attachments is what is needed again at this later stage?

This isn't an argument for no boundaries, no honesty, no authenticity. It is a belief in the benefits of being reliable, consistent, and attached. It means figuring out what this other person might need and trying to offer it; it means accepting what happens as, well, just what happens while staying 100 percent committed to figuring out how to get to a loving place. It means that no matter how much our children irritate us by behaviors we cannot understand and do not wish to accept, we must hold to the intention of making it work better at some point in time.

Love Is Not Finite

I have talked before about my wonderful young friend in her thirties, married with two toddlers. In talking with her about this book, I saw a perspective quite different from my own. "Susan," she said, "your audience is not me. I am not really so interested in what my mother-in-law thinks. Frankly, I don't think much about it. You know, my husband is now mine. I live with him. He loves me, and there are more critical things to worry about than how my mother-in-law feels."

Her comment was sobering. *"He is mine!"* Her little boy is only one. It will probably be more than two decades before some other young woman might think, "He is mine now. His mother will just have to deal with it."

Are my daughters-in-law thinking just that? "He's mine! He loves *me*. His mother is yesterday's spaghetti."

Good heavens.

Okay, let me sort out truth from emotions here. He *is* hers. He is fully hers, I hope. He does love her. I hope he loves her passionately and intensely, and she returns those feelings. And I clearly understand that does not mean he can no longer love his mother, or that he is no longer mine. He will always be mine, be ours, as well, as having their own children will help to make clear. He is not mine the same way he is hers. We are not in competition here. If they can have a great marriage, it will be excellent. If they can have a great marriage in the context of a warm and loving extended family, it will be more excellent. I am voting for more excellence.

When I was a young bride, I didn't think about how I wanted to relate to my in-laws. Now that I look back, I probably shared the "He's mine!" mentality. I remember my husband's parents letting us know that they were not enamored of the sixties sideburns I had encouraged, and my thinking that it didn't matter what they preferred because I was now playing on the center stage. Really, it didn't matter what they thought about sideburns. But it did matter, with the wisdom of hindsight, what we thought about dealing with our parents.

When Dysfunction Overrides Good Intentions

How do good and decent people end up in unpleasant family situations? First, it is important to acknowledge that, sadly, some children are self-absorbed, inconsiderate, or plagued by poor judgment. Some mothers and some fathers are destructive forces. They are selfish, punitive, abusive, greedy, and, on occasion, dangerous. They do hurtful things and they do them again and again.

I have read many stories from young mothers, and the stories of in-law relations are sometimes quite awful. One distraught wife wrote that her mother-in-law, who had a perfectly fine apartment of her own nearby, spent months camping out on the sleeper sofa in their living room, eating their food, and demanding to watch the television programs she preferred. Certainly, this mother-in-law had "issues," but I found myself thinking the crux of this problem rested with her son who was unwilling to confront his mother, set limits, and support this wife. There are many circumstances when the challenges are far greater than how a mother-in-law fits into changing circumstances. These are family systems problems and require more intensive efforts than described in this book. I know that every situation will not yield to good intentions and a loving heart.

Every normal family has "dysfunction." Odd is normal. Problems are normal. Conflicts are normal. What isn't normal? Physical abuse of any sort is not normal. Persistent, intentional humiliation is not normal. Continued refusal to comply with clearly stated wishes that are judged reasonable by a wide range of people who really know all the facts is not normal. Behavior so intrusive as to deny sexual, emotional, or financial privacy is not normal. If toxic behaviors are so familiar that they have begun to seem normal, it really is time to go to the balcony, probably with someone else who can help decode what is going on. Sometimes, just a few visits with a skilled therapist can help us reframe how we are looking at a situation and how we might handle it with better results.

What I am writing about in these chapters does not apply to people who are consistently destructive. Some heartaches we must simply hold. Sometimes, there are family members who must be cut loose. If in-laws are a danger to our children, are persistently disrespectful and demeaning, if they hurt us physically or intentionally demean us emotionally, there may be no choice but to disconnect. But don't go there quickly or easily. My own rule of thumb is: don't do anything you would not one day be willing to have done to you.

Just what that means can be complicated. A woman who is a gifted artist and curator, and looks about fifty, is now in her seventies with a serious illness. She talked about her own search for when to give up. This woman has led an interesting and expansive life, but it does not include a daughter, who refuses to speak with her.

> I understand why she is so angry. My mother didn't know how to love me, and I didn't know how to love her when I was younger, and then her father was

stricken with cancer and died. I was angry. She was angry, and anger became our cup of tea. Now she is still very angry with me. I so want to fix it, to apologize for whatever I need to apologize for. I did the best I could, and it wasn't good enough. I get that, but I am going to die, and she is going to be left with all that hot anger, and I wish that I could lift it from her.

The daughter, now in her fifties, is committed to her anger. Having only the mother's side of the story, we don't see a full picture, but what psychology tells us is that until this anger is released into something less bitter, it is likely to spill over into other relationships. Sometimes we carry very old angers, old hurts that we have not forgiven even decades after the event. Without understanding what is going on, we can project this anger onto unrelated situations. A few words, a minor event, can trigger in us old pains that we then play out in new situations, blindly. This is where a dose of good therapy can help. The therapist has a better chance of watching from the balcony and helping us see the patterns that are invisible from the floor. And sometimes good friends can play the role of therapist. When our friends or even our partners tell us we are not seeing so clearly, it is a good idea to stop, breathe, and listen.

It is *My* Story, and I'm Sticking to It
We have just been talking about individual patterns, but we also can be caught up in cultural patterns. Can the fish tell us it is in water? Culture has clout. It tells us a story, and we think it is a true story. The wife of our older son is from a Chinese immigrant family. Her parents came to the United States more than thirty years ago and sent five children to college, although her deceased father never spoke English, and her mother barely does so now. They were modern in their ambitions but traditional in their customs. This daughter-in-law, who has been married to our son for eight years, has always called me, as I asked her to do, by my first name. A few years ago, she told me her mother chided her still for that.

"What does she think you should call me?" I asked.
"She thinks I should address you as mother-in-
law." "But did you tell her I asked you to call me
Susan?" "Yes, of course," she said, "And she said,
'What does she know?'"

I love this story because it so perfectly hones in on our convic-
tion that what we expect is what we believe is *correct*, right, just, and
we judge others negatively when they stray from our vision.

I have a close friend who is a gifted life coach and works with
high-powered executives to help them understand the narratives they
live in that undermine their effectiveness. With a highly tuned ear
for stories, she is able to see the difference between her mother's story
and her mother-in-law's story and make sense of her own mother's
actions.

My husband's mother has five children. Whenever
anyone gets married, her story is that this is as an
opportunity to bring a new and interesting person
into the family circle, a chance to have fun with one
more person. My own mother has a story that our
marriages bring loss, something that will take her
children away from her and disrupt the routines
that are already established.

The consequence is that my friend finds visiting her mother
difficult and demanding, and puts it off as long as possible.
Nothing is ever quite right. My friend is told that she doesn't
come often enough, call enough, pay enough attention. But she
loves visiting her mother-in-law who always makes her feel special
and interesting.

Certainly, the cultural patterns in which we swim are different for young women than for young men. It may be the twenty-
first century, post feminism and women's liberation, yet many
parents feel there must be a man who will take care of their little

girl. This is a belief that runs deep into the land of expectations. If mothers assume the "best thing" is for women to have children and stay at home with them and be provided for by a steady and loyal husband, and the daughter and/or her partner have a different expectation, trouble is at hand.

If a son or son-in-law cannot provide for his family at the same level as his father or father-in-law did, is the young man failing? If a woman is the major source of family income, is she carrying an unfair burden? Should women be expected to contribute to the family income if needed, even when there are small children? What is the obligation of parents toward adult children? Is it unfair that our children spend holidays at a lovely resort as guests of the other in-laws and never with us?

There is no key of "right" answers to these questions. But if parents think they have "right" answers, and the answers don't align with what is, in fact, happening, and if they convey with words or body language displeasure, tension is sure to follow.

For professionally successful women, it can feel disrespectful to be told a husband should provide for them. For women who want to work or need to work, a mother or mother-in-law's disapproval of this just adds to the difficulties of leading a complicated life. For a husband, whether son or son-in-law, being out of tune with parents simply encourages retreat. "I can't see the point of fighting about something I can't change," says one young father. "I just don't engage in conversation. My mother-in-law thinks I'm cantankerous, but I think I'm self-protective. If I opened up and told her how much it upsets me to see her upsetting my wife, it would not be pretty."

How often do we mothers and mothers-in-law ask ourselves when we complain about some circumstances, "How is this complaint influenced by expectations I brought to their marriage that they don't share?" A retired psychologist heard the daughter of a friend talking about the "allowance" that her husband gave her. "If that were my own daughter, it would drive me mad." Another is bothered by her daughter's willingness to let her husband dominate decision making.

Conscious or not, mothers often expect their daughters will be like them. And they hope their daughters-in-law will be like them as well, like them in values and life styles. Why? Deborah Tannen's explanation makes sense in my own life. Women, she explains, value inclusion. From the time they are little girls, they fear being left out. Inclusion for many women means talking and sharing experiences.

> A daughter who moves into worlds her mother does-n't inhabit moves away, creating a distance more unbridgeable than the physical distance of moving to another city ... Although it doesn't always turn out that way, it seems that sameness ensures closeness, and differences lead to distance.[2]

Mothers most often want to be part of their children's adult lives, and when those lives travel to unknown places, mothers can become scared that they cannot travel with them and will be left alone and lonely.

The problem is that this is a conundrum difficult to see and to articulate. Instead it gets disguised in berating comments, put downs, "poor-me" whines. What if we expected that our children would be, metaphorically, traveling to foreign ports, and our job was to follow their travels and understand the new cultures they were visiting as best we could?

A few years ago, my husband and I decided to visit Africa. "Why Africa?" my mother asked. "Do you like animals? What's so great about Africa?" This strangeness she can discuss. But it is harder to be so direct about the strangeness she sometimes perceives in my work life, my marriage, my housekeeping, my child rearing. So it comes out in odd and often annoying ways. I tell her this book has just been bought by a publisher, but I will have to work very hard to finish it by the deadline. She says, "Why are doing it; do you need the money?" Twenty years ago, I would have felt irritated at her insensitivity and lack of joy for me. Now, now that I know how to decode better, what I hear her saying is "Are you still going to have enough to time to be here for me? That's not what I would do. Why aren't you how I expected you to be?"

Here is what I am learning about my married children and their lives: I don't have to like it. I don't have to understand it. I don't have to approve. I just have to know that the decision is really *not* mine. And I have to remember that we didn't want our parents making our decisions. Why should it be different when we are the parents?

I also have come to see that I don't always get the balcony picture. My son tells us it would be better if we didn't visit for Labor Day. We had carefully planned our schedule to permit this visit, and we are disappointed. What he doesn't share are the conversations with his wife about her desires, plans, concerns. These are private, and he doesn't invite us into their private conversations. I'm on the floor and have no idea how it all looks from up above. I am thankful that I have gotten to the point where I know there is another angle, even if I don't see it.

Because women so often speak a language of feelings and inclusion and men more often use a language of acts, it happens that women can feel more comfortable talking to other women. Some-times, that means that mothers-in-law don't often address their sons-in-law and sometimes even their sons directly. For the first ten years of our marriage, my mother would address all ques-tions about my husband's preferences to me, even when he was sitting on the couch in full view.

> "Susan, do you think Michael wants ice tea or Coke
> with lunch?"
> "Michael, do you want ice tea or Coke?"
> "Neither. Just water is fine."
> "Okay, Mom, he just wants water."

What was that about? Why was I complicit in having my husband reduced to a puppet? I could have, should have, helped them address one another without my needing to be the puppet master.

Over coffee on a vacation to the desert, the mother of an only child confessed her difficulties relating to her new daughter-in-law. When I shared my own realization that I had been communicating with my son and not including his wife on e-mails, she said,

> Yes, but I don't know her e-mail or her cell phone. My son got through my divorce with his father by carefully separating his relationship with each of us. He saw his job as ensuring harmony, and so he never spoke about either of us in the presence of the other. I think he fears there will be friction with his wife, and so he wants me to go through him to communicate.

The son, unaware and with all good intentions, was helping his wife and his mother to stay unconnected, and it took an on-the-balcony conversation to realize that the conversation this mother needed to have was not with her daughter-in-law but with her son. He expected that his role was to ensure harmony. His mother went to work helping him expect that they would all work out a healthy relationship. When a child marries, we have to make a psychological shift. We have to move from the singular to the plural. Our son or daughter is now part of a *we*. Instead of calling, e-mailing, writing to him or her, we must communicate, most of the time at least, with them.

Sons Only

"I wonder if someone you interviewed had any anecdotes about daughters-in-law naturally gravitating to their mothers when those relationships are good, and thus the son's mom gets somewhat left out?" wrote a friend after reading an early draft of this book. *Yes*, yes, yes, is the answer. We have already touched on this a bit, and on situations in which the son's family exerts the larger gravitational pull, but more than one woman spoke the old saying, "A son's a son 'til he takes a wife, but a daughter's a daughter all her life."

"My son and his wife both grew up here in Houston," explained a woman who echoed other stories about competition among in-laws. "The children visit us often, but they always stay at her mother's house. My daughter-in-law is just more comfortable there. I understand that, but wow, it hurts." Another spoke of always being invited by out-of-town in-laws to visit with them for holidays. "I appreciate their caring to include us. But sometimes I wish I could be the one doing the inviting, or that I could just have these young people to myself. When I try to say something, my son explains how much his wife likes going home. What am I going to do?"

It would seem that living in the same city would make family events easier, and often it does, but when the in-law families don't get along as easily as their children do, the same pushes and pulls appear. It helps to work at uncovering what really bothers us. For example, we are bothered because it doesn't seem fair that ... , etc., ... And why does that bother us? Well, because it feels like we are the losers? And why does that bother us? Because we don't like that feeling? And what can we do to get rid of the feeling? Oh, well, there it is again ... it is about us not them.

I understand that there are exceptions to what I'm going to say—and hurrah for them—but mothers and daughters are more likely to go shopping, have lunch, run out to look at a pedestal sink together than mothers and sons. Sons and fathers might continue to share an interest in sports, and yes, many mothers are sports fans as well. But the mothers of sons seem to speak more than the mothers of daughters of a need to have occasional alone time with sons. "I miss my son," said a friend. "He's a terrific, funny guy who is very much on my wave length. I like his wife, and I enjoy seeing him shape his own family, but how much I would like to have some time with him alone, not because I have any special message. Just because he is my son, and I miss being with him."

There are many uncomfortable stories of mothers who expect their sons to be their handymen, gardeners, or companions, who invite their sons to come for meals and make it clear the wives are not expected. This is not, of course, what I am advocating. It is a gift when our sons, and also our daughters, can help us; it is not a right.

"Wait," a young friend corrected me. "It's not like you say at all. I am not keeping my husband away. My husband cannot abide his mother. I do him a great favor by protecting him from her." Well, maybe. Maybe one reason the mother is irritable is because she knows she is being avoided and shunted aside. This is a pickle, and it may be the favor is not so kind. Having unhealthy attachments with parents makes it harder to have healthy attachments with our own children. If we parents care about our grandchildren, we should care about trying to heal any wounds with our children. I don't think this necessarily requires going back and reliving the past and delving into what went wrong. Wishing for a better past is not productive. It isn't going to happen. Whatever went wrong before, we can start trying to do what is right today and hope it allows us, in time, to forge a better relationship.

If you are on the floor, in the action, and damn sure you understand what is going on, but your spouse and your best friend and a couple family members are on the balcony disputing your version of events, you are ripe for a time-out. Sometimes it is hard to realize that what we are doing is not going to get us to where we want to go. In these moments, we have to allow others to disrupt us and help us reorient. Robert Quinn, whose quote starts this chapter, writes about transformational change. His focus is larger than the family, but the advice is applicable: "The transformational change agent says, 'Here is the standard, which I know looks impossible. But let's stand together and we will learn our way into a higher level of performance." ❧

What Do You Do When You Suspect Disaster Is About to Strike?

THIS YOUNG DUBLIN FELLA COMES HOME ALL EXCITED TO TELL HIS MA HE'S FALLEN IN LOVE AND GOING TO GET MARRIED. HE SAYS: "JUST FOR FUN, MA, I'M GOING TO BRING OVER THREE WOMEN, AND YOU JUST TRY AND GUESS WHICH ONE I'M GOING TO MARRY."

THE MOTHER AGREES, SO THE NEXT DAY HE BRINGS ALONG THREE BEAUTIFUL WOMEN AND SITS THEM DOWN ON THE COUCH, AND THEY CHAT AWAY FOR A WHILE. HE THEN SAYS, "RIGHT, OKAY MA, GUESS WHICH ONE I'M GOING TO MARRY."

SHE IMMEDIATELY REPLIES, "THE ONE IN THE MIDDLE."

"THAT'S AMAZING, MA. YOU'RE RIGHT. HOW DID YE KNOW?

"BECAUSE I DON'T LIKE HER."

– Found on Internet joke site

Why *That* Person?

Go looking for books on in-laws and you will find lots of them happy to promote the idea that mothers-in-law are jokes. Obviously, that's not this message, but I borrowed this joke because it points to a very difficult issue.

Yes, there are mothers who adore the sons-in law their daughters chose, and mothers who believe their sons made wonderful decisions in the women they married. When luck is at work, parents are delighted. If not delighted, many are accepting with quiet reservations. Ah, but, sadly the categories continue and include (a) concerned, (b) critical, (c) perplexed, (d) hostile, or, in rare cases, (e) disconnected.

What happens to slide us into one category or another? The cheap answer, of course, for all categories but delighted and accepting is, "My child made a bad choice." And sometimes, our children do make bad choices. "My college roommate gave me a frying pan for a wedding gift with a note that said, 'I hope you only need this for cooking,'" remembers a young woman from Michigan who is now happily divorced. Obviously, one child has already married or stands on the brink if you are reading this book, but it is likely for many readers that other marriages are yet to follow. And the discussion for giving advice about marriage surely applies as well to divorce. What do you do when you see your son or daughter headed for what appears to you to be sure-shot disaster?

Even harder question ... How can you be sure what disaster is? In a friend's midwestern family is a story about a beloved aunt who was head over heels in love with a charming, impecunious beau who was "artistic" and planned to take both of them to Hollywood to make movies. Her relatives were appalled and trip-wired what they considered a ridiculous relationship. They steered her into the hands of the Princeton-educated son of a local businessman of considerable wealth ... an agreeable young man who, it turned out, had an affection for gambling and none for hard work. The charming beau did go to Hollywood and was a fabulous success, while the Princeton scion ran a struggling shoe store with a lively poker game in the back. No telling how marriage to the first would have evolved, but we do know that predictions of the future are a risky business. Does that mean parents must always *keep their mouths shut* when they want to say,

> ... He's got a nasty temper ... She spends money with no concern for what's available ... She complains all the time. Nothing ever seems right ... He's unedu-cated ... has no table manners ... doesn't keep his promises ... She's lazy ... sloppy ... cold ... The family's health issues are a matter for alarm.

We have observations, predictions, worries. And then, some-times, we see perfection, and yet, it is not to be. I am thinking of my friend's friend who married the ideal Ivy-League MBA, on the investment banking fast track. With a lovely wife, two cute kids and a big house, he lost himself in alcohol. I know a young man who married the scholar-athlete, a star in her college years, who developed obsessive-compulsive disorder as a young mother. These illnesses were unimagined. I talked with a mother-in-law of the sweet young thing who only years later decided her mother-in-law was a witch-in-disguise, and one who told me about her agreeable son-in-law who suddenly decided his children never needed to visit his wife's parents. Such behaviors were unpredictable. Oh, the misery the world has squir-reled away in corners waiting to drip away on us. Don't we want to save our children from as much misery as we can? Isn't that part of our job as parents?

We Don't Have a Veto. Do We Have a Vote?

I don't struggle with whether or not I should try to help my chil-dren avoid misery. I am genetically wired to do that, whether or not someone else thinks it is appropriate. What I struggle with is know-ing when and knowing how and knowing when not. When are my values good values for my children, and when are they just some-thing I acquired for me but not something that has any extended warranty? Is misery for me no big deal to others?

Before we have to wrestle with how to be a good in-law, do we have any say in whom our children marry? Well, no, we really don't have much say, but I don't believe that means we should ignore loudly broadcast warning signs of trouble when they assault our senses. However, if we tell a child, "Do not marry this person," and they do anyway, you can be sure your relationship with the new spouse will start out rocky, very rocky. You know your child is going to speak of your unhappiness and it won't be forgotten. And if we tell them *don't*, and they don't, what is to keep them from regretting our advice ever after? What to do?

Here is what might help. I think we may be honest with our children about our concerns. That is very different from telling them what to do. Admit our fears. Admit as well that we just don't know what makes love work nor what the future will bring. Admit that when you love a child, you so much want good things for him or her. Work very hard on making sure that is the truth. If no one ever seems good enough for your child, the problem may not be the child's choices. A young economist confides,

> My brother is an Ivy-League educated lawyer, captain of the ski team in college, all around great guy, and he's depressed. My parents never think any woman he brings home is good enough. He talks to my mother all the time. She still buys his socks and his underwear. My parents should have encouraged him to marry the woman he loved who was of the "wrong" religion and let him blossom into a man instead of the wimp that's emerging.

If you feel you simply must have a conversation with your child about his or her choices, be willing, from the very start of this conversation, to have any outcome at all. Be committed to the process of conversation but not to a specific outcome, for example, that you are going to derail a relationship. Admit that sometimes parents don't always see things objectively, but note that if this is true, it is probably also true that children, even adult children, don't always see things objectively. Further recognize that who the hell knows what "objectively" means in this context. A friend spoke of a man who married a young woman who was losing her sight. His parents were terribly upset. They could not understand why their handsome and capable son would want to live his life with a woman who was disabled. But the son considers his marriage a daily joy. This woman is his soul mate. She completes him and he, her, and together, they have a happy life. I heard from woman who, at nineteen, fell head over heels in love and married her beloved on his way to a Mexican prison for drug possession. They fathered a daughter while he was in prison completing a five-year sentence. You can imagine her parents' reaction. Today, they have been happily married for thirty years, and her parents adore their son-in-law, an outcome that defied all their reasonable expectations.

If you really feel strongly that your child is embarking on a perilous course—which goes way beyond wishing for a mate with a different religion, profession, or pedigree—talk about an idea you once read in a book, this book, in fact. Here is the idea: Any one person may not see the whole picture, but if you ask a team of people, people who are generally unbiased and usually of good judgment, for their opinions, the consensus point of view is likely to have merit. So, before committing to marriage, how about committing to asking four or five or six people who have insider information, people besides the parents, what they think. If your favorite aunt and your college roommate, your colleague at work and your beloved's sibling are all telling you this marriage really does not seem like such a good idea, well ... hmmmm, maybe you should pay attention and consider some premarital counseling. If there are mixed results, maybe you want to slow down the process 'til you have more information.

Libido or Love

The reason to marry someone is because we love being with the person. He or she helps us become our best self. It is fun to be together. Getting married because young people cannot wait for physical intimacy any longer makes it hard to figure out whether someone is really going to help us be our best self. Urging children to marry to avoid sex before marriage or to legitimize what they are already doing seems dangerous. Needn't we be careful that a desire to place sex inside marriage does not lead young people to mistake hot for heart and end up in situations that are unsustainable over time? Do we want to teach young adults that if you do sleep with someone, the honorable thing to do is marry them? Isn't it honorable only to marry someone you love and want to build a long and full life with, and to marry because it seems to be right for you both—not because it is right for the other's parents or your parents?

I am always surprised when a woman tells me—and I have heard this many times—that she knew walking down the aisle that she was making a mistake. Perhaps men sometimes feel this way as well, but it is the women whom I hear saying it. In any event, one thing we can do to help prevent disaster is to let our children know that when in doubt, don't. No catering bill, no matter how big, no fear of embarrassment, justifies marrying to save face or money.

Helping Children Get Perspective
Although we may not always see the world as our children do, that does not mean I think young people shouldn't listen to their parents. They should. As a card-carrying member of the Medicare generation, I can say with assurance that we learn lots by living. If we are awake, we get wiser as we get older. I do know things I didn't know at thirty, although I felt a lot smarter at thirty than I do now. Our children should listen, with an open mind and a loving heart, and think very hard about what they hear. But because we are older, and we are parents, and we have seen some stuff, it does not guarantee that we are right. One good way for young adults to listen to parents is to hold the question: What would make my parents' point of view correct? What makes them think this way? This is also a very good way for parents to listen to children. And, oh dear, we should go first.

What makes for a good marriage? I doubt that it is growing up in the same faith, although that certainly helps. I doubt that it is having the same skin color, although that can make life easier. I doubt it is knowing the same crowd of people. Common backgrounds allow a couple to communicate in a kind of experiential shorthand, but all of this can be addressed. My guess is that it has to do with sharing common values.

Do two people see work as holding the same kind of place in their lives? Do they share similar views on children and how to raise them? Is their approach to money and how to spend it and save it compatible? Do they have a similar understanding of the role of family in one's life? Do they want the same kinds of things in life? Do they agree about what is ethical, what is fair, what is funny? How can young adults answer these questions? It is not likely that many will explore them with their parents, which is why premarital counseling is such a good idea. Encourage them to explore these questions with someone else ... and don't ask "So, what's happening?" if they are sensible enough to do so.

And, if you see disaster looming, but your son or daughter sees hearts and harps, this is painful; but you have to love them enough to stand with them and to be there if things don't work without ever saying, "I told you so."

Finding Perspective Ourselves

An article headlined, "My Child's Divorce Is My Pain, " talked about the financial burdens some parents take on when a child divorces, the sadness and disappointment the parents can feel, and the sense of guilt when they believe their own behavior contributed to the failed marriage in some way.[1] None of us wants to see our children hurting, but causing them to think that their actions are hurting us as well adds difficulties to something that is almost always already difficult. And what if our child's bad behavior is the cause for the divorce? Isn't that the time to pull out the lines we were taught when the kids were toddlers: "I love you but I don't love what you did. You are not a bad person, but I see this as bad behavior."

Recently, I was chatting with the woman next to me on a plane ride. She was coming back to Houston from a visit with her fiancé, a man of whom, she explained, her mother disapproved. The disapproval focused on two things, the fact that he was divorced and was a Catholic, rather than a Baptist. "But you just told me you were divorced," I observed.

"Yes, I am divorced, and he's warm and loving, and cares about my two children, and has encouraged me to start my own business because he's willing and able to support us. You would think that would be enough, huh?" She then went on to explain that she had been one of those women, walking down the aisle, who knew she was making a mistake. After a few years, she told her parents she was contemplating a divorce. They told her it was completely unacceptable, that she had made her choice. "So, I decided this was my lot in life, I had my two children, I brought in most of the money, I ran the household, and we hardly had a sex life, but I thought this was it ... until I just couldn't stand it any more."

The rest of the conversation made it clear that her parents certainly loved her and wanted good things for their daughter, but they had an unfortunate ability to give what seemed to me to be questionable advice: Stay married to a man who uses you, but break it off with a man who loves you and wants to care for you but is divorced and of the "wrong" faith. So here is where we as mothers need to do the very thing I suggest for our children. We need to get the advice and counsel of others whom we respect but who have different perspectives. When we are a friend who knows our friend wants empathy, sympathy, understanding, do we lecture them? It isn't kind to say, "I think you are wrong," but it may be kind to say, "Do you think there is another way of interpreting this?" We need to hear how other parents and other young people interpret the stories we are spinning. And if all of our friends tell us, "Give it up," well, we must give it up.

Since there is no way of knowing whether our dire predictions will come true or, blessed with good fortune, all will be well, there is nothing wrong with being prudent about protecting your interests and those of your children. If you are giving your children money to buy a house or start a business, it is not unloving to treat it as a legal transaction. The reason we have contracts is not to tell us what to do in the best of circumstances but how we must behave in the worst of situations. One father wanted to help his daughter with a small house for her growing family. The father is a housepainter and was able, with the help of friends, to take an inexpensive fixer-up and turn it into an attractive home. But he judged the house to be sturdier than the marriage. Instead of giving the couple the house, he retained the title and asked the young couple to pay a modest rent which was deposited in a fund for the grandchildren. Sure enough, when the husband departed, this young mother was able to stay in her house.

Not for all of us but for a great many, it is hard to see problems and not want to speak about them. It is also extremely dangerous to talk. When people are in love, they talk about everything, and that everything usually includes what parents say. Hone in on the perceived faults of a prospective new family member, and you may find you have created an adversary who doesn't forget over time. If you absolutely can't stay quiet, you must be very careful. Instead of observing that, for example, the beloved one seems to be a spendthrift with extravagant ways, you might note that this person seems to have different ways of approaching money than your family, and note that, in your experience, this can turn out to be a contentious issue in a marriage, and would it be productive to meet with a financial counselor now to work out the different perspectives? If you get blown off, you raised the issue and got strong feedback telling you it was not going to be received.

We may find certain behaviors intolerable, while our child may decide he or she can live with this and prefer to let it slide rather than dealing with the consequences of making it an issue. There is only one situation in which I feel sure it is wise to step in and that is around abuse. Here local or national hot lines can be a first place to look for advice and support. I spoke with only one woman who had direct experience with this, although I know from serving on the board of the Houston Area Women's Center that it happens far more often than most of us suspect. What the woman whose daughter was being abused said was, "This situation broke my heart. My daughter loved this man. I came to hate him. It took seven years for her finally to leave, and it felt like one hundred. If I came on to her too strong, she just retreated and lied to me. I simply had to be there until she had had enough."

Sometimes, people make mistakes that allow them to learn lessons they need to learn. When the children were little, we knew that. We let them make little mistakes in the service of their growing up. Marrying the "wrong" person is hardly a "little mistake," but this growing up turns out to be a lifetime's work. If you do decide you are going to take the chance to speak out against a union, make sure the issues you chose are worth the risks at hand. If the marriage has occurred, and you see stress cracks, let your child know you are there, always. Mothers who have tried to offer advice without being asked report that it more often hurts the relationship than helps the child. We think we are criticizing a partner, but our children can hear it as criticism of them. Sometimes, children may be cool to our concerns, not because they don't see the concerns, but because they just don't want to "go there" with us ... and we need to allow them this freedom.

One woman, who is watching her son in a very difficult circumstance, said, "I used to want to know what was going on. I didn't ask, but I was there to listen and would ask a follow-up question. Now, I try to avoid these conversations because I think my son has no good choices. I don't know what the best choice for him and his family is, and I don't want to feel I pushed him in any direction."

Because our children so often care deeply what we think, and because our thoughts have great power to hurt them even when it isn't our intention, it is far safer simply to make clear our love and respect and stop right there. Honoring an adult child's judgment is one of the most loving acts we can offer.

In *Anna Karenina*, Tolstoy wrote, "All happy families are alike; every unhappy family is unhappy in a different way." The ways difficulty can sneak into our lives are endless in their variation. How do we manage our role as a mother-in-law and, perhaps, grandparent, when a child dies or commits a crime? How do we handle drastic and unanticipated changes? What is our responsibility in the face of serious chronic illness? I did not speak with many women facing such difficult circumstances, but one woman said something that seems deeply wise: "The hardest thing I have ever had to learn is that I cannot take my child's pain from her. She is separate from me, and we hurt in different ways. I must respect her pain, and I must also respect my own; they are not the same. No matter what awful thing happens, life goes on, and for that I want to remain ever grateful."

CHAPTER SIX

Making Sense of Annoying Behaviors

THE VOYAGE OF DISCOVERY IS NOT IN SEEKING NEW
LANDSCAPES BUT IN HAVING NEW EYES.

– Marcel Proust

How we behave rests on our deepest assumptions about how we think the world should operate and how we believe it does operate. Reducing a very complicated subject to the most simplistic level, how should you slice a pizza? Most of us will say in pie-shaped wedges. My friend Barry is going to say in squares, even though the pizza is round. "The rest of the world is wrong about this. Pizza is better eaten with our fingers, and small squares are so much easier to eat than droopy pie slices," Barry asserts. His assumption about the right way to eat pizza makes most pizzerias in the world wrong. Talking about this with Barry makes me laugh, but there are lots of people in my family and my life who have deeply held assumptions that don't leave me laughing.

For example, some of us operate on the assumption that candor is a gift and by saying what we think, others can know how we feel and respond more fully. Others feel candor is abrupt, rude, and confrontational, and it is not helpful to say everything we think. Some think it best that we reveal nothing of what we think.

About half the people in the world get energy from engaging with others. These extroverts are engaging souls who like to chat, visit, and call on the phone. They talk to think and often work out their ideas aloud. The introverts among us find that social interaction takes energy and need to limit socializing to have time for the quiet reflection that fuels them. They want to think things through before they talk. Who is right? Of course, there is no "right," but when introverts leave the dinner party early or refuse to come at all, extroverts can feel hurt. When extroverts ask a dozen personal questions in an effort to engage, introverts can feel violated. My husband, the only introvert in our immediate family, used to complain at the dinner table that he couldn't get a word in, and by the time he could, we were three subjects down the line. These differences, some inborn and some learned early and wired into us, can turn into irritations.

There are many ways to center ourselves and resist being aggravated by what we think are the misguided acts of our children, their spouses, and other family members. What has helped me is learning about type and temperament research. I was first introduced to this when I was working for the Rural Practice Project in Chapel Hill, North Carolina. My husband had come to North Carolina to work at the National Institute of Environmental Health Sciences. I was at home with two toddlers on a cul de sac with no sidewalks, no bus service, and no activity but for the mailman at 1 p.m. I was moving straight into lunacy and knew I needed a part-time job to save me from becoming really witchy.

Understanding Type and Temperament

The job I found was with a Robert Wood Johnson Foundation-funded project to maintain rural medical practices when the young doctors who were working in rural areas to pay off government loans completed their obligations and left the community. The head of our project was an intensely private but passionate man who heard about something called the Myers Briggs Type Indicator (MBTI) and decided our small staff could benefit from learning about this MBTI.

All seven or eight of us took the MBTI assessment. I remember thinking that it was the dumbest set of questions I had ever been asked to answer. Then, some weeks later, the reports for each of us arrived. I don't know why they ended up on my desk. I should not have seen them before they were given to each participant, but I didn't know this when I opened the packet and read them. I was stunned. They were dead on in describing each of us. Then Dr. Mary McCaulley, then the head of the Center for Psychological Type, came to explain it all.

What a huge gift this has been for me for over three decades. The MBTI doesn't explain everything there is to know about a person, and it isn't *the truth*, but it has been a powerful tool in helping me to understand why other people do what they do and why I do what I do. The MBTI isn't the only personality assessment instrument. Since first finding myself intrigued by this Jungian-based work of Isabel Myers Briggs and her mother Katherine Briggs, research on personality types and meaning-making models have held my attention.

What's a meaning making model? A recent op-ed piece by David Brooks offers one example:

> The world can be divided in many ways—rich and poor, democratic and authoritarian—but one of the most striking is the divide between the societies with

an individualist mentality and the ones with a collectivist mentality ... the individualistic countries tend to put rights and privacy first. People in these societies tend to overvalue their own skills and overestimate their own importance to any group. People in collective societies tend to value harmony and duty. They tend to underestimate their own skills and are more self effacing when describing their contributions to group efforts.[1]

In families, some members value the larger family over individual needs, and when they encounter relatives who put the individual first, there is often judgment—or, worse, anger. How we distribute family resources, how we share work, how we spend time, and how we think about all of these is influenced by our deepest assumptions about making meaning.

Whether we value religion and ritual or not, whether we take risks or avoid them, whether we find competition or opportunity in changing circumstances depends on our usually unconscious patterns of thought. It is natural to feel someone else is wrong when they behave using a different operating system. Did you ever use the word processing program Word Perfect? It was the system I first learned when I began using a computer, and I have always found the way it operated to be superior to Word ... but Word has become the industry standard, and Word Perfect has faded. My personal preference had to give way to widely shared conventions.

Sometimes in family life we have to adjust to fit the personality or the majority preferences of the family. One of my favorite Thanks-giving family traditions was to play charades after dinner. I assumed it was fun for everyone. It hit me, hard, to realize that I was the only one who really wanted to continue this. We no longer play charades. I've recovered. If you value tradition and believe rules matter, and your offspring suggest the family celebrate Thanks-giving together the first weekend in December, it may feel very wrong and even hurtful. If, on the other hand, you place more weight on creativity and adaptation than tradition, you may

judge your child clever and imaginative. It is so hard to walk in someone else's brain. But having a little understanding of the different
ways people process helps.

Take in Information. Make a Decision. Repeat …

I have worked with various personality assessments including the
DISC, the Birkman, and the Enneagram, and I know there are
others. Here, I'll use the MBTI, which I know best, as a reference
point in talking about how inborn differences shape our behaviors.

The MBTI says that we go through our lives taking in data and
making decisions based on the data. You know, you get up in the
morning, take in the time on the clock, and decide whether to get
up or hit snooze. You drive along the freeway access road, take in
the traffic flow, and decide which route to take to work. The
MBTI doesn't tell us how good we are at data collection or at
making decisions, but it does tell us about the way we like to collect
the data and make the decisions, ways that shape our personalities.

Some of us take in data concretely. We taste, touch, smell, feel,
count. We are tactile and fact based. We like to start with the what
is (**S**ensing). Others of us don't begin with what is but what could
be (**IN**tuition). We prefer theory to data. We get hunches, visions, inti-
mations. It isn't that data is unimportant, but it gets processed, not
as details, but as possibilities. A factually-oriented family member might
tell you she is buying a new Prius, and then give you the mileage per
gallon, the safety record, the cost comparison, and the repair
record. An equally enthusiastic Prius buyer with a different way of
taking in data might begin by explaining that buying a fuel-efficient
car is the responsible thing to do, it is a car that is right for the times,
it will benefit the environment, and it is going to serve her lifestyle
well. Not a number in the pitch, but lots of ideas.

Knowing these different styles explains why some people want
the details first and others like to begin with the vision. People
who like the details get impatient with what they consider pie-in-
the-sky. Before they can contemplate the virtues of a vacation to
Morocco, they want to know how much the plane fare costs, what

the weather will be like, and what the State Department has to say about terrorism. Others wonder why it makes sense to bother about any of this until you finish imagining the various virtues of a Morocco trip versus Turkey versus Disneyland.

Once we take in information, we move to making decisions based on the information. The Myers-Briggs model says some of us begin in our heads, using rational, logical processes (**Thinking**). Others of us go first with our gut; we start with personal values, with what feels most important (**Feeling**). Make no mistake here. The coolly logical thinkers also have feelings, and those who start with emotions can analyze and organize as well. People just start in different places and work the process in different ways. The first group can seem cold and calculating to the second, who, in turn may accuse those not like them of being overly emotional or irrational. One way does not lead to better decisions than the other, but they do not travel the same paths to arrive at the destination. Along the way, we are at risk for insisting our path is the "right" way.

What Gives Us Energy?

There are two more aspects of the MBTI. In addition to the two "functions" of taking in data and making decisions, the instrument says we have two "attitudes" that influence the way we manage data and decisions. The first attitude is Introversion or Extroversion. This does not tell us how well we do at cocktail parties. It describes where we get our energy. Extroverts are energized by events in the outside world. Introverts draw their energy from going inside themselves. I consider an evening with friends a great way to relax. I am energized by the conversation and laughter. My husband, who has a strong preference for introversion, finds such evenings work, even when they are entirely enjoyable. "But Susan, Mike can't be an introvert. He's so funny and warm," friends will tell me. Yes, he is funny, and he is warm, and he's highly skilled in social situations, but they never give him energy; they take energy.

The extroverts in our extended family think sitting around the breakfast table 'til it's time for lunch arguing and chattering is a great way to celebrate any event. The introverts, more given to reflecting or doing than talking, think that is weird. The extroverts talk to figure out what they are thinking. Don't hold them to what they say while thinking aloud. The introverts think to talk. Don't push them for a response until they have time to consider what they really believe. They may not like to be surprised and at first resist ideas that come out of the blue. The person wired for spontaneous impulse, for socializing anywhere and anytime, may judge the other dull and staid, while the more reflective of the two wonders just how this strange relative is put together.

A Preference for Exploring or for Deciding

The second attitude tells us whether in our interactions in the world, we prefer to take in the data (**P**erceiving) or make the decisions (**J**udging). Obviously we all do both every day. We couldn't drive to work if we didn't make decisions, and we couldn't navigate the traffic obstacles if we didn't take in data. MBTI describes what our default positions are likely to be, what we prefer to do.

Some of us are eager to come to closure. We want to make a decision and move on. Others of us enjoy gathering information, reflecting, piecing together the facts. Both are useful. If we know what we prefer and what others prefer, it helps to move from "What's wrong with him ...?" to "Oh, we have got a temperamental difference playing itself out here ..."

The research indicates that until we are firmly rooted in our preferred ways of being, it is more difficult to begin to develop our less-preferred ways of being. As we get older and more at ease with what we already do easily, we can develop our less-natural skills—but first we need to develop what we most like. This gives us mothers-in-law an advantage. We are more able to move across the scales, more able to learn how to take in data and make decisions in ways that are not our natural inclinations. In *The Female Brain*, Dr. Louann Brizendine notes that post menopausal women are less reactive to stress and less emotional. We may not have as much tummy tone, but we may have a hormonal edge on our daughters and daughters-in-law that allows us to consider type differences with more calm and consideration than we might have a few decades earlier. More importantly, we may have a hormonal edge over our younger selves.

No type is better than other types. In the world, we need all the skills collectively described here. Certain circumstances may favor one set of preferences over another, but all are useful in the world. We all have strengths, and we all have blind spots. A healthy family wants to be able to use all the strengths it has at hand.

There is a very good chance our children have types different from ours, and that the people they marry will be other types still. If one of your children or their spouses is an introvert and you are an extrovert, you may find they don't chat on the phone as much as you would enjoy. For introverts, chatting is not a favorite thing. They have only so much chat available, and it must be measured carefully.

Men and women who prefer the concrete and have a deep knowledge of how things have always been, value tradition and may be strong family loyalists. They find comfort in mastery and maintaining a steady pace. Others in the family, more like me, would revamp the shape of the egg just for the challenge. The future, the possibility of creating the new, holds our attention far more firmly than the what is. Chaos is stimulating. Multitasking is normal. We must be careful to see the preferences of others as inborn differences, not character flaws.

If extroverts talk to think and introverts think to talk, it can be easy to step on toes. And if one of us prefers to begin with the facts and another starts with the possibilities, is it any wonder we frequently confuse each other?

What's more valuable, our head or our heart, our left hand or our right leg? There are personality styles we prefer. But there isn't one way that is better than another. Some styles are better suited to certain activities. You wouldn't want an accountant who glossed over the details or a surgeon who said, hmmm, let's just try something different for the fun of it. But you wouldn't respect an architect or artist who only looked to the past, a chef who never followed a hunch, an entrepreneur who didn't decide to challenge common wisdom. We can't change who our children are. We can't change who we are. I like the MBTI because it gives me a language to explain my discomfort. "Hey guys, you know I, who like closure, have trouble hanging out without a decision all day. Can you pick a time by which we will decide, so I can let go of my compulsion to have completion?" When my husband checks out in the middle of the afternoon to take a walk alone, we all understand he needs to replenish his extroverting supplies before dinner.

If everyone in the family but one person shares a preference for one of these four functions or attributes, that lone soul can be made to feel "wrong." In fact, the family needs his or her perspective because it lights up a different corner.

The MBTI is just one of many instruments that categorize and describe human behavior. They are all imperfect. If I lined up twenty executive types, my preference, they would not all seem just like me, and there is much about me you still do not know even with my MBTI letters. But if you know my type and know the theory, you are less likely to see my behavior as personal and more likely to see it the same way you see my shortness or my sixty-year-oldness or my femaleness.

It is hard, really hard, to understand others. Think how hard it is for them to understand us. So, we meet this new person at nineteen or twenty-seven or thirty-four, and they say, "I do," and we are supposed to treat them like family. We are supposed to love them and understand them and support them. And we want them to do the same for us. How do we make that happen?

Working toward Intimacy

Learning something about type is one powerful way to work on reducing feelings of distance in our families. Women around the country have suggested some others. This story comes from a retired lawyer who is never thought of as shy by her friends but who found herself uncomfortably quiet with her son-in-law.

I had to force myself to talk, I mean really talk, to my son-in-law. You know how women chatter and men trade sports facts? It hit me one day that in six years, I had never really had a conversation with my son-in-law. I knew my daughter loved him, but I wasn't sure why. I knew I couldn't just go up to him and say, "Jeff, let's start talking," but what I did was stop using my daughter as a proxy. When I wanted to know something about his work, I would ask him. And if I didn't understand, I would tell him I needed more explanation. And then I would tell him how much I appreciated hearing this from him. I would ask him questions about their children. I didn't even tell my daughter I was doing this because I didn't want him to feel like he was part of an experiment. I just did it, and it didn't turn things around immediately, but after a couple years, we just fell into a more comfortable way of talking.

One young woman noticed that using her parents as a place to complain when she was in a bad mood affected the way her parents dealt with her husband.

My mother and I are close, and she is a safe place to vent. When something is worrying me or I'm upset with my husband, I use my mother as a sounding board. That's good, but I've come to see that it has a bad side effect. Long after I'm finished worrying about something, my mother is still fretting. Instead of telling her how great my husband is and how much I love him, I end up talking about some momentary money worry or some annoying glitch we encountered, and she sees him as less terrific than he really is. I have made a conscious decision to stop using my mother as a release when I am grumpy.

While this comment is from the daughter's point of view, we mothers are wise to remember that when our children screamed, "I hate you," they didn't mean it, and often, when they grumble, it may be just a passing mood.

When I was a young mother, I had a wonderful neighbor down the street whose children were grown and with children of their own. Each year, she and her husband took the whole family on vacation. What interested me was her reasoning.

> When the girls come home, they revert to their sixteen-year-old selves. It is much better to gather on neutral territory. Everybody has private space to which they can retreat, including me. And I don't revert either ... to the person who does all the cooking and cleaning and washing. We all come as grown-ups, and most of the time the grown-ups act their ages. I also find it is helpful to choose really wonderful, lush places. Our children lead busy, complicated lives, and it's hard for them escape. If we pick places so nice they can't say no, it doesn't feel like an obligation, and they are eager to come. We pay for everything because we don't want money to impede our getting everyone together.

Here is a version of the same story from a woman who doesn't have the same financial resources but does have the same impulses.

> When my married children come home, I work very hard to make it a lovely time. I cook all their favorite foods. I put flowers in the bedrooms. I have candles and candies. We babysit and insist they take time alone with their spouses. I want to make coming home something really wonderful so they want to come and like being here. I never pick a fight while they are here if I can help it. And one night, when we

are all together, we have a little family ritual. After dinner, we go 'round the table and do catch up. Each person explains what they are doing in their lives and what's new, interesting, troublesome. While the guys might not do that one-on-one, somehow the group thing seems to get people to talk, and it works. I learn stuff about the kids every time.

Still another woman who loves playing poker manages to host a monthly poker game for her son, her son-in-law, and their friends.

I'm the only woman, although the girls are welcome, but they babysit for the children. Because I'm so much older and not a guy, I seem to become invisible at these games, even though I play and play well. They talk and joke among themselves, and I often learn something about what is going on with them. I never mention it. I just let them think I'm putting out the food and cards as a favor to the girls, but really, it is a favor to me. 🐾

THERE ARE NO CHOSEN ONES

The MBTI, with its four bimodal scales, describes sixteen different MBTI types. Each of the types have characteristics that often show up in people with this personality preference. Each type has been given a descriptive name:

Duty Fulfillers (ISTJ)

Serious and quiet, interested in security and peaceful living. Extremely thorough, responsible, and dependable. Well-developed powers of concentration. Usually interested in supporting and promoting traditions and establishments. Well-organized and hard working, they work steadily toward identified goals. They can usually accomplish any task once they have set their mind to it.

Mechanics (ISTP)

Quiet and reserved, interested in how and why things work. Excellent skills with mechanical things. Risk-takers who live for the moment. Usually interested in and talented at extreme sports. Uncomplicated in their desires. Loyal to their peers and to their internal value systems, but not overly concerned with respecting laws and rules if they get in the way of getting something done. Detached and analytical, they excel at finding solutions to practical problems.

Nurturers (ISFJ)

Quiet, kind, and conscientious. Can be depended on to follow through. Usually puts the needs of others above their own needs. Stable and practical, they value security and traditions. Well-developed sense of space and function. Rich inner world of observations about people. Extremely perceptive of other's feelings. Interested in serving others.

Artists (ISFP)

Quiet, serious, sensitive, and kind. Do not like conflict, and not likely to do things which may generate conflict. Loyal and faithful. Extremely well-developed senses, and aesthetic appreciation for beauty. Not interested in leading or controlling others. Flexible and open-minded. Likely to be original and creative. Enjoy the present moment.

Protectors (INFJ)

Quietly forceful, original, and sensitive. Tend to stick to things until they are done. Extremely intuitive about people, and concerned for their feelings. Well-developed value systems which they strictly adhere to. Well-respected for their perseverance in doing the right thing. Likely to be individualistic, rather than leading or following.

Idealists (INFP)

Quiet, reflective, and idealistic. Interested in serving humanity. Well-developed value system, which they strive to live in accordance with. Extremely loyal. Adaptable and laid-back unless a strongly-held value is threatened. Usually talented writers. Mentally quick, and able to see possibilities. Interested in understanding and helping people.

Scientists (INTJ)

Independent, original, analytical, and determined. Have an exceptional ability to turn theories into solid plans of action. Highly value knowledge, competence, and structure. Driven to derive meaning from their visions. Long-range thinkers. Have very high standards for their performance, and the performance of others. Natural leaders, but will follow if they trust existing leaders.

Thinkers (INTP)

Logical, original, creative thinkers. Can become very excited about theories and ideas. Exceptionally capable and driven to turn theories into clear understandings. Highly value knowledge, competence, and logic. Quiet and reserved, hard to get to know well. Individualistic, having no interest in leading or following others.

Doers (ESTP)

Friendly, adaptable, action-oriented. "Doers" who are focused on immediate results. Living in the here-and-now, they're risk-takers who live fast-paced lifestyles. Impatient with long explanations. Extremely loyal to their peers, but not usually respectful of laws and rules if they get in the way of getting things done. Great people skills.

Guardians (ESTJ)

Practical, traditional, and organized. Likely to be athletic. Not interested in theory or abstraction unless they see the practical application. Have clear visions of the way things should be. Loyal and hard-working. Like to be in charge. Exceptionally capable in organizing and running activities. "Good citizens" who value security and peaceful living.

Performers (ESFP)

People-oriented and fun-loving, they make things more fun for others by their enjoyment. Living for the moment, they love new experiences. They dislike theory and impersonal analysis. Interested in serving others. Likely to be the center of attention in social situations. Well-developed common sense and practical ability.

Caregivers (ESFJ)

Warm-hearted, popular, and conscientious. Tend to put the needs of others over their own needs. Feel strong sense of responsibility and duty. Value traditions and security.

Interested in serving others. Need positive reinforcement to feel good about themselves. Well-developed sense of space and function.

Inspirers (ENFP)
Enthusiastic, idealistic, and creative. Able to do almost anything that interests them. Great people skills. Need to live life in accordance with their inner values. Excited by new ideas, but bored with details. Open-minded and flexible, with a broad range of interests and abilities.

Givers (ENFJ)
Popular and sensitive, with outstanding people skills. Externally focused, with real concern for how others think and feel. Usually dislike being alone. They see everything from the human angle, and dislike impersonal analysis. Very effective at managing people issues and leading group discussions. Interested in serving others, and probably place the needs of others over their own needs.

Visionaries (ENTP)
Creative, resourceful, and intellectually quick. Good at a broad range of things. Enjoy debating issues, and may be into "one-up-manship." They get very excited about new ideas and projects, but may neglect the more routine aspects of life. Generally outspoken and assertive. They enjoy people and are stimulating company. Excellent ability to understand concepts and apply logic to find solutions.

Executives (ENTJ)
Assertive and outspoken — they are driven to lead. Excellent ability to understand difficult organizational problems and create solid solutions. Intelligent and well-informed, they usually excel at public speaking. They value knowledge and competence, and usually have little patience with inefficiency or disorganization.

From www.personalitypage.com, written by Brenda Mueller and reprinted with her permission.

———————

The is much more to understand about the Myers Briggs Type Indicator than is presented here. If you are curious, here are four of many good books to explore as well as a book recommendation for the Birkman and for the Enneagram.

Recommended Reading
to Understand More About MBTI

1. *Please Understand Me II,* David Keirsey
2. *Just Your Type: Create the Relationship You've Always Wanted Using the Secrets of the Personality Type,* Barbara Barron Tieger and Paul Tieger
3. *MotherStyles,* Janet Penley
4. *I'm Not Crazy, I'm Just Not You,* Roger Pearman and Sarah Abritton

Other Explanations of Personality Assessments

1. *True Colors: Get to Know Yourself and Others Better With the Highly Acclaimed Birkman Method,* Roger W. Birkman.
2. *The Enneagram: Understanding Yourself and the Others In Your Life,* Helen Palmer.

CHAPTER SEVEN

When Our Babies Raise Babies

HUG O'WAR

I will not play at tug o'war.
I'd rather play at hug o'war,
Where everyone hugs
Instead of tugs,
Where everyone giggles
And rolls on the rug,
Where everyone kisses,
And everyone grins,
And everyone cuddles,
And everyone wins

– Shel Silverstein, Where the Sidewalk Ends

We were pleased, really pleased, that one of our offspring was going to make us grandparents. At sixty-five and sixty-six, it seemed we were among the last among our friends who expected grandchildren to have them appear. But my pleasure was tinged with a shadow of sadness. I knew that the time we had with our adult children would change. It could be years before we would ever really be alone with them again. If I was still working on being a good mother-in-law, now I was going to focus on being a good grandmother as well.

So along came this adorable baby and, well, he was a little boring those first few months, lovable but not very interesting for someone who thinks the teens are the best age for children. This charming child has now gotten more interesting, but what really grabbed my heart was not the baby. It was our son and daughter-in-law with their son. Just after the baby was born, I heard a line from Proust describing a piece of music. That line hit me as the perfect expression of what I was feeling. Watching our son with his son "made an indelible stain on my mind." The pleasure our son and his wife took in being parents was sweet beyond measure. But the sweetness had a hint of bittersweet.

We went to visit when the baby was just a week old. I sat in the living room, watching our son and his wife with their baby, and I physically felt, deep inside me, a tectonic shift. The baby slipped into his role as representative of the next generation of the family, of the children's generation. My son and his wife moved up the ladder from children to parents. They took the center of the stage in the generational diorama, and Michael and I slid down the rails and occupied a new spot as, well, as the old folks. No, of course, our sons don't quite think of us as "the old folks," but they don't think of us as the young folks either.

This isn't bad. It just is, but it is a bit odd because it is new casting. If this boy graduates high school at eighteen, I will be eighty-three and, perhaps, the nice old lady being helped to her chair—if I'm still help-able. Who the hell is *that*? If ever a thought got me off my duff and to the gym, it is that one.

Tell a friend you have just become a grandparent, and odds are you will hear "Congratulations!" What do those heartfelt congratulations mean?

Since so many grandparents talk with such deep pleasure about their joy in having grandchildren, certainly part of what people must be saying is, "Oh good for you. Now you are about to have something very enjoyable in your life." Perhaps another part of the message is more reflexively evolutionary: "Hurrah for your family that your genes just made it into the next generation." Maybe it is an indirect salute to your children, a toast to their procreative good fortune.

I have heard parents say, "Parenting is not all it's cracked up to be." I have yet to hear a grandparent complain about being a grandparent. There must be some scoffers, but the bewitched majority have clearly scared them into silence. Adults of all types seem to love being grandparents. I don't think my husband carried a picture of our boys when they were young, but he amazed me by pulling out a photo of his brand new grandson at the airport for people we barely knew. Grandchildren, (unless you have had to take on the parent role yet again) my friend Ellen explained, are all joy and fun without the responsibility. "You get to be the good fairy, and someone else has to play the heavy this time." When our son was still a boy himself, maybe eleven or twelve, he made me promise one night at bedtime that when I was a grandmother, I would spoil his children. "A grandma has to love her grandchildren and give them cookies and not tell them they are doing anything wrong." He, who loves his own grandmother, seems still to think this a proper role, and I don't mind … unless his wife minds.

But, odd as this may sound, I always hear a bit of a warning behind the congratulations. The warning isn't from the giver of these good words but from my own brain, reminding me that this new kid on the family block is my grandchild, not my child. This time around, when I actually have some experience and wisdom, I am not going to call the shots unless it is with a camera.

We got to do it our way with our own children. They get to do it their way. Yes, we know we made mistakes, and we want to help our children avoid them. Of course, we have opinions about child rearing and, better yet, we have hard-won experience. What we don't have is license to meddle. Even when meddling feels like a good idea. Even when it seems clear to us that a few wise words well heard could do wonders. Even when our kids are, in our eyes, making a botch of it.

These are examples of the kinds of things grandparents talk about away from their children:

> My daughter loves her children, but she feels guilty that she is working, and she and her husband get home late, so she lets the kids stay up way too late, and she is far too permissive, and the result is that her kids are often annoying brats. They whine because they are tired and because it works. Then she and her husband feel stressed because the kids are so whiny.
>
> ...
>
> Yes, I have offered advice, but I do it very carefully, always as a suggestion, never as a directive. I see that my daughter already feels a bit defensive because the kids are not as well behaved as others in the family and the last thing she needs is to have me, her mother, make her feel like she is not a good mother, since she already doubts herself.
>
> ...
>
> My son-in-law is too rough with his sons. What is supposed to be play too often ends in tears. He wants it to be fun, but the little one clearly isn't having such a good time. My daughter sees it but can't talk about it in a way that can be heard. If she can't be heard, what are the odds I'm going to be heard?
>
> ...

I think my grandson has a learning disability. His parents are in denial. They desperately want him to be A-OK. They would rather make me out to be the wicked witch than think their little boy isn't perfect. What am I supposed to do?

...

My daughter-in-law has gone nuts. If I pick the baby up without a clean cloth on my dress, she thinks I will infect him. You can't make a noise when the baby is sleeping. His schedule rules the roost, and there is no flexibility. I feel so bad for my son, but he allows all this for the sake of peace.

...

Is bedtime really too late in the first instance, play too rough in another, and problems apparent in a third? Are rigid schedules really so annoying? Are the parents off the mark or the grandparent? Where the heck *is* the mark?

When my own sons were very small, I noticed that if I asked the pediatrician a practical question to which he didn't know the answer, he would tell me what his wife did. That didn't mean, of course, that it was what I should do. I was twenty-nine when I had my first child. I wanted to go back to work part-time, and I asked my kindly, old fashioned doctor about pumping and storing breast milk while I was away from home. He responded by saying, "You waited long enough for this baby. Don't you think you should stay home and take care of him for now?"

I was shocked by the answer. He meant well, wanting the best for me and the baby, and his best judgment, based on years of practice, led him to think I didn't need to go back to work. There was no evidence, at least none he was offering. He just felt that way based on his intuition.

Many mothers and mothers-in-law talk about having similar

feelings, not so much about working mothers but about why certain things are right or wrong. Television is not so good. Reading aloud is excellent. Saturated fats are evil, but a little bit of dirt builds up immunity. These are my biases—all of which may seem inane to someone else ... and therefore I want my grandchildren to have benefit of what is right, don't I?

I have to keep remembering that pediatrician, whom I abandoned for his sureness that ran counter to my own needs. I also have to remember my grandmother, who would not sew a button on anything I was still wearing unless I held a piece of thread in my mouth because, in her world view, it invited evil. Or my own mother, who believed that if she told me, "Nobody will notice from a galloping horse," it would make me feel better that the shoes didn't really match the dress, when I knew perfectly well it was *not* okay.

Mothers and mothers-in-law can be wonderful sources of advice. We know our children, and we know our grandkids, and we understand the context, and we come with experience. We can, equally, offer terrible advice. After all, we probably haven't raised a baby in some years, and perhaps we only know part of the story and do not see the whole context. So, whatever we may want to say, we can't offer our advice unless we are asked. If we politely ask, "May I offer some advice," the person asked sounds hostile if he or she says, "No." Or they say, "Yes," and they are thinking, "Hell, no." "You just have to wait," counsels one very experienced woman. "If you are quiet, when things get bad enough, they are likely to ask for that advice."

If you feel, however, that you are not going to follow the "Keep your mouth shut" rule, and you do not have the needed restraint to resist the overwhelming need to give advice, at least remember the following:

> Don't offer in the middle of the crisis.
> Don't offer in front of others in the family.
> Don't offer when an adult child is already upset.

Don't offer when we are upset.

Don't offer with the expectation that because we
    say it, it will be so.

Don't offer with a critical voice.

Don't offer without love, respect, and understanding.

A capable woman in San Diego says, "I am learning to ask permission to speak out ..., Gee, it has been a long time since I had young children, but maybe it will be useful if I tell you what I remember from my experience ...' Then I pause ... wait for an expression, even a weak one, of interest. No interest ... I talk weather." A young mother disagrees. "Don't offer advice. Period. Offer play dates, recipes, money, food. Ask if there is some way you can help. Smile. Go home."

What we can say without permission is all the things we appreciate (but *not* as a checklist against the list of things they are *not* doing right in our eyes). "My relationship with my daughter-in-law got much better, one woman explained, when I consciously started telling her where I had been wrong." Our children and their partners are old enough not to need our advice, but they are never old enough not to need our affection and approval. My daughter-in-law is, by my lights, an excellent mother. She is organized, informed, and not neurotic. She loves her son but lets us share. She has a schedule, but it is flexible. And when I tell her this, I believe it matters to her. She does so many things well that I never thought to do. And if she does some things I would not do ... what difference does it make? They aren't harmful to the baby or to me or to them. Let go, let go, let go, goes my grandmantra.

Intimacy at a Distance

By 2010, there will be more than eighty million grandparents, and about forty million will live more than two hundred miles away from the grandchildren. How do we get to know our grandchildren and have them get to know us across space? Fortunately, technology has come to the rescue. Recently, I figured out how to use the iMage camera sitting on top of my computer so we could communicate through Skype in three dimensions. There is the baby and his father waving. "Show Nana how you learned to pull yourself up," his dad directs. So the baby rolls over on the floor instead and smiles, again and again and again. It is very cool, even if standing must wait for another video session. His mom is great about making 30-second videos she sends by e-mail that allow us to enjoy his developmental progress, and, in time, I aim to learn enough to send our own videos back when he can comprehend.

It is fun for me to shop for the baby and for my daughters-in-law, but when I send clothes, I try to send them from national chains so they can be exchanged. I may send clothes with the tags still on, suggesting that the parents exchange whatever doesn't seem just right.

We are always willing to babysit when we visit so our children can have an evening alone. It's funny that they seem to think it odd we don't want to eat with them. They also seem to find it odd that we drop in and drop out fairly quickly. I am following the advice of the mother of three married children living in cities all distant from her. "I have come to believe that frequency is good but only if the duration is short. I come, I smile, I go." If you must pay for a plane ticket or for gas, the cost is the same to you whether you visit for three days or three weeks. In most instances, three days is enough time to catch up and begin to become an imposition. Certainly, if your children invite you to stay for longer periods of time, and then they repeat the invitation, they might mean it. If they need your help, and you are willing to give it, by all means do what makes sense. But remember that if schedules and sleeping conditions are disrupted by your presence, it can put a strain on the most loving children. We must take our cues from them.

Perhaps your children seem to forget to invite you to visit. You may decide just to surprise them. Please, don't. Even if you have a key to your child's house, a good rule of thumb is never to enter without an invitation or a call, and never to walk in without ringing the doorbell unless you have specific instructions to do so.

For ideas about how to interact with grandchildren, the Web, of course, is full of resources. A site I like that lists other sites as well is http://www.grandloving.com. It isn't sensible to try to be any "cooler" than we are. We need to do what we do, and then invite our grandchildren to join us, join us in watering the plants, setting the table, cooking, reading, walking. "My kids remember the real things they did with their grandparents long after they have stopped talking about the spectacular things we did," one young mother tells me when I worry about entertaining grandchildren.

If you are fortunate enough to spend time with your grandchildren, there are some wise caveats that parents bring up again and again. Building from them, there is a list of behaviors you really don't want to own. If your children or other family members suggest you are falling into one of these traps, resist the impulse to deny what you hear. Pay attention. It is easy, for example, to find you prefer one special grandchild or to say things that are not appropriate for kids to hear. You are the grownup, and you must put a stop to your own behavior when it is out of line. Here are some problem areas younger parents wish that we would avoid:

> My parents criticize my spouse to my children.

> When my kids complain to my parents about our disciplining them, our parents side with the kids.

> The grandparents know the rules we have, but they purposely ignore them and undercut us.

> We ask the grandparents to avoid certain foods, and they "forget."

> The grandparents compare our child to his cousins in hurtful ways.

> My in-laws give our children too much and too soon. Their gifts are not age appropriate and sometimes dangerous.

> My parents don't like one of our children, and it is quite clear to all of us. This is so painful that I put as much distance between us as I can.

And, much more cheerfully, here are some of the things parents of younger children report they cherish about grandparents:

> They make our children feel special and cherished.

> I know playing games with the kids can be tedious, but they are so patient and cheerful and the kids just melt—as do I.

> My mother-in-law is incredible about not making judgments. If my daughter shows her a picture and says it is horses, my mother-in-law doesn't comment on the quality of the horse ... good horse, funny horse ... she just talks about horses generally. "Wow, you drew a horse," Or, "That's certainly a horse."

> Our parents always ask us if what they are planning for the grandchildren feels right to us.

> When I am at my wits end and think my kids are terrible, my mother-in-law says, "Oh, I so understand how you feel," and doesn't offer me advice.

> My in-laws speak to our children like real people. They listen to what they say and ask thoughtful questions. They don't talk down to them, and the children respect them, even the littlest, for this.

> We are a gay couple. Our parents never behave as if we, or our children, are in any way different from our heterosexual siblings.

> My mother understands that a treat is what my daughter wants, not what my mother wants.

There is much more that can be said about grandparenting, but the focus here is on the relationship we want to have with the grandchildren's parents. They are the parents. They are in charge. They are in charge even when we think they are wrong. Sometimes, the ways our children raise their children get in the way of our relationship. Mothers have spoken of daughters or daughters-in-law who have such rigid schedules or food rules that the grandparent feels anxious and constrained. This discourages their visiting and impacts their relationship with both their grandchildren and children. "My daughter is a food nazi. If I give my grandson a taste of candy and he mentions it, I am castigated. I think she is nuts, but I try to follow her rules and not teach my grandson to lie to his mother. Still, I sometimes want to give a little candy. He loves little cars, so, instead, I spoil him with these." Another complains about the rigidity of feeding times. "Six of us can be out together, and if it is time for the baby to eat, we all have to go home, ready or not. This baby doesn't get snacks in the stroller to 'spoil his appetite.' We all think the parents are crazy. The parents *are* crazy. They are our crazies."

No Babies

And what happens if we expect to be grandparents and there are no grandchildren? We have to wait to be told the circumstances. We cannot tell our children we think it is time they make babies. They know how to do it, and they most likely know what we think. If they are having trouble conceiving, pressure from us will only add to their woes. If they are having trouble deciding what they want, it is a decision only they can make. And if they choose not to have children, it is not our place to agree or disagree—at least not aloud. &

CHAPTER EIGHT

Fixing a Mess

NOTHING IS A BIG DEAL. IT IS WHATEVER IT IS,
AND THEN IT'S SOMETHING ELSE.

– Sylvia Boorstein , *It's Easier Than You Think*

Sometimes, oh damn it anyway, we just get it all wrong. We say the wrong thing. We act dumb as a donut. We misunderstand and act as if we understood. We lose our tempers or worse, our good sense. It happens. Odds are it happens to you. And to your children. And to their children.

I was going to write, "Don't despair," but despairing seems an appropriate response when you realize you blew it, and you don't want it to be like that. So go ahead and despair, but while you are doing that, breathe those deep yoga breaths ... four beats in, one beat holding, six beats out, and again and again.

Okay, so you've breathed and you still feel bad. Hopefully, you are just a little more centered from the breaths and can begin to plot a way out of the mess. Writing about this has forced me to think about my own messes and how I respond, and to talk with others about their messes. I've come to some conclusions, and they have helped me, so maybe they will help you.

First, we have got to figure out what really is going on with *us*. Why we say we are losing our tempers is not always really the honest reason. Until we can figure out what is eating us, we aren't going to get control of it. For example, one seemingly-together woman had to come to grips with the fact that she was picking on her son and daughter-in-law for a whole variety of unimportant things, when what was really bugging her was their decision on religious direction for their young son. "But I can't talk with them about religion. I know it's their choice, and I have no right to interfere, but it bothers me so much, and so it keeps popping out in inappropriate ways."

So if the first step is to identify the real problem, the second step is to figure out how to talk about it. It may be that the talk is not with your children but only with yourself or with a friend, a therapist, or a religious leader; but it's got to be someone who doesn't tell you, "Look here is how you should think about this," but who can help you figure out for yourself what you are thinking, what is eating at you, what the consequences are, and does it really matter?

My husband and I are Jewish. Neither of our sons married women who are Jewish. I don't know how they will raise their children. I'm not sure they know because our needs and choices can change over time. Yes, my husband and I care a little. It would be difficult for us if we had a grandchild who grew up learning that our chosen religion was anything less than just fine. It would be nice if our grandchildren shared our religious traditions—but if they share ours then they may not share those of their other grandparents. For sure, I know there is something wrong with a set up in which people end up feeling like winners or losers.

What matters for us most is that our children and their children are healthy and happy, and the parents are unified in their child-rearing decisions. Since I don't get to call the shots on this issue, why let it be divisive? So, for me, the crux of distress is not, perhaps, religion, but my inability to exert the control I seem to like. The issue, now, is not their behavior but mine.

Now the "rules of behavior" get murky. Some of the mothers and mother-in-laws with whom I have talked believe that it is far, far wiser to keep silent and not raise these issues at all. "What is the point?" observed one mother who deals with significant religious tensions. "Nothing I say is going to change anything, so why say anything?" Another woman insists that it is better to share one's concerns and hurts. "I don't expect to change things, but just in the way my children want me to know how they feel, I want them to know how I feel." Equally important is that we try to find out how they feel. If we can be openly and honestly curious and appreciate our children's desires to find a spiritual path that satisfies, we can share in their journey.

If we are going to talk about our feelings because we cannot resolve them in silence, we have to do it the same way people were taught in the seventies to discipline children. None of that, "You are a *baad* boy" stuff. We learned to say, "You are a good boy, but writing on the wall is a bad thing that you cannot do." We learned to say, "It bothers other people when you shout, so please talk in a normal tone of voice," rather than screaming, "You cannot shout. Stop it now." Now we can say, "It is painful for me to deal with this or that, so can you help me figure out how to get comfortable with this?" We can say, "I really struggle with this decision of yours, and since I can't find a way yet to let it go, I think we need to avoid it for now." We can say, "I'm sorry I have so much trouble with this and this and this, and I'm working to make my peace with it, so please be patient." Or we can stop looking for resolution, for shared understanding, and plant a vegetable garden or hook a rug or volunteer at a homeless shelter and just let the tides of time wear down our spikiness.

I think all mothers-in-law need to be a little Buddhist along with whatever else they are being. Buddhism teaches the eightfold path with these signposts: Right Understanding, Right Aspiration, Right Action, Right Speech, Right Livelihood, Right Effort, Right Concentration, and Right Mindfulness.

I don't have to be a practicing Buddhist to pay attention to an explanation of Right Speech: " ... making sure every single thing [I] say is both truthful and helpful." Happiness is a choice, my choice. It doesn't mean I have no pain, no disappointment, no sadness. It does mean that I do all I can and then let go of fixating on what I cannot change. We can attach to caring, to working, to holding our visions clearly in front of us. But what is the point in being attached to specific outcomes when we don't have control over all the inputs, and when, so often, it doesn't really matter.

Some years ago, I participated in an Interfaith Seminary program. I heard a line in seminary that I love: Refusing to forgive is to remain committed to a better past. The other one-liner that makes me laugh every time I repeat it is: Hanging on to resentment is like taking poison and expecting the other person to die.

When we have made a mess, when we have walked a wrongfold path, we must apologize. A daughter told me about a mother who drank too much and then apologized for ruining family events and was upset when her kids stopped accepting the apologies. Simply saying I'm sorry and then repeating the same behavior doesn't cut it, of course. What this mother needs to be sorry for is not upsetting another dinner but for her inability to deal with her alcoholism. That's the real issue and that, she may be truly sorry about. Whether her daughter can understand and accept that sorrow, I don't know, but it is the more fundamental regret, isn't it?

The consequences of such behavior are that she is now often excluded from family gatherings. Is it fair? I don't know about fair.

I know that what we do has consequences, and if others don't like what we do, they do what they do. We can say, "Well, I don't care," ... unless we do, and then we have to ask what role we can play in making things better.

Mostly, our messes are less chronic, less difficult than chronic alcoholism, but even small difficulties can require some action from us. If we hurt the feelings of an in-law, we can't apologize to the spouse, our child, and ask them to "Pass it on." We have to apologize directly to the person who merits the apology.

Now, of course, you are thinking it should work both ways. If *you* have to apologize when you screw up, don't the children need to do the same? Ah well, that's a theoretical position. It is not one, I have decided, that is worth holding to in practice. Expect no apologies, and you will never be disappointed. Act like you got one, and whatever the fight was about, it's over. Just keep being cheerful and nice. Why, you ask? Because the consequences of this tactic generally make for a cheerier outcome than any other. Would you rather be right or contented? I know someone is already asking, "How can I be contented when I have been done wrong?" Oh, just let it go. I know, I know ... it is easy to say and harder to do, but I, the queen of justice and fairness, have come to believe that it isn't worth holding on to grievances that don't make anyone happy. I'm not talking here about truly outrageous behavior. It is never a good idea to be demeaned and dismissed and come back for more.

That said, I must confess that in order to let go, I have to indulge in a certain amount of whining and complaining to expiate my sense of injustice. I wish I could let it go more easily, but I am not always there. For this, my husband is of great use. After the whining, he usually tells me to give it up, I get angry, leave to sulk, realize he's right, and, well, give it up. Really, that's about the way it works, and the whining and sulking get shorter all the time. I hope for more and more progress! 🐾

CHAPTER NINE

Building Family Traditions

Combat the sense of pressure that discourages us
from taking time to celebrate, the sense so many of us
have that we cannot stretch our time or energy one
more notch, by opting for simplicity. Small moments,
little gestures, can have a powerful impact.

– *New Traditions*, Susan A. Lieberman

I wrote my first book twenty-six years ago. I was forty and
living in St. Louis. That book, *New Traditions: Redefining
Celebrations for Today's Family*, is still in print. It evolved out of
our move to a city far from both sets of parents. There I was, alone

in the kitchen cooking up a dinner of traditional holiday foods for the four of us, only to have my children go, "*Eeeew*," after which I found myself with a pile of dirty dishes and no celebratory spirit. I wanted our children "to grow up with Technicolor memories," and I wanted the same for us, but I wasn't sure how to create them. I cried in the dishwater. As now, I wished for direction, for good ideas, and started asking everyone for input. The result was a kind of cookbook but not for food. Rather, it was a series of "recipes" for ways people adapted, reinvented, or created anew special family times to suit their own circumstances. It was so interesting to do and influenced our own family in wonderful ways. Now, every time I suggest something, someone in the family may pipe up, "So, Mom, should that be a new tradition?"

Family traditions work on several levels. First, they shape our family recollections. They give texture and color to being Smiths, O'Connors, Correllis, Cantus, Kolowskis, or Cohen-Wongs. Second, they signal when the family will be gathering. We know in advance when we need to make time for family. Third, they simplify our lives. We don't have to figure out what to do for celebration. We know what we'll eat or wear or say, and the rhythm of repetition has a comfort and ease to it that makes honoring certain moments or events easy. People just know when and where to show up, and, often, what will happen. … We'll grill hot dogs and hamburgers, take out the boat, fish and tell ghost stories when it gets dark. Or we will all come to Mom's for dinner, and there will be our favorite foods, and each one of us will report something great about the year past …

Traditions set expectations. That's the good part. I can count on knowing my whole family will show up for Thanksgiving. That's also the bad part. When unexpected events, say, send one contingent to North Carolina for Thanksgiving for the *other* family celebration, it is easy to be really disappointed. We may have had family traditions for more than a decade, and then circumstances change. Here's the creative tension: we have to honor our traditions and commit to keeping them alive; we have to be willing to alter our traditions and adapt them when they stop giving the family shared pleasure. While tradition does focus our attention on "What do we do?" I think the overarching questions we want to hold together are these: What do we want to achieve with this celebration or activity? How can we best get there for all of us?

It's a great idea to agree on some family traditions that work for everybody and remove the need for always negotiating. And it is an even greater idea to be flexible and understand that the unanticipated happens, times change, needs morph. I have this crazy conversation that sometimes goes on inside my head. One voice says, "We are getting older, and the kids need to bend to our needs and our schedules." The other voice says, "Hey, we are the ones with time and flexibility, and they are the ones with young children and jobs, and we need to bend to their schedules." Both are true.

I sometimes want to honor the first voice, but I know I need to pay more attention to the second while my husband and I enjoy good health and are able to navigate easily. My life is busy but theirs is busier still. I may love having the children "come home," but they love having us appreciate the home they are making. After a couple decades of holding center stage and arranging things on my terms, that act is over, and their lives have to take center stage. I am not the leading lady ... just in a supporting role. Do I like it? Not always. Never mind. I suspect there will be yet another revision when our children are again better able to travel, and we may be less able. And what if no one can travel? Can we be creative and have shared moments long distance? Can we all watch the same movie, or read the same book, or try out the same recipes and feel connected emotionally?

It is interesting that nearly three decades later, I find myself wanting to revisit and review the ideas in *New Traditions*. I have now reached the moment when it is time, again, to recalibrate for our family. I think it may be wiser now not to start out proclaiming a tradition but just to propose something for the moment and see if it roots and grows. Here are some ideas that adapt to this mother-in-law stage of parenting.

When the children were young, we came up with a template for the eight nights of Hanukah to be a counterforce to rampant materialism. Each night had a theme: big gift night, small gift night, mommy night, daddy night, giving night, poem night, food night, word night. When our sons were in college and away for this holiday, I started sending them Hanukah boxes using the same idea: big gift, small gift, joke gift, magazine subscription, food, art, wearable, music. Friends have borrowed the idea for Christmas, adapting it to their own family preferences. One friend suggests the box be used for the Twelve Nights of Christmas and not compete with Christmas morning. Others intend for all the gifts to be given in one large box. When the boys married, I started including their wives. Either each of them gets a personal gift, or they get a shared gift. Soon, we'll include grandchildren. The gifts are seldom extravagant, but I hope they are seen as thoughtful. I am always on the lookout for just the right things to drop in the boxes.

One large, dispersed family contributes sums to a family travel fund instead of giving gifts, and every five years, they have a large family reunion at a great summer camp facility and use the money to offset the travel and lodging costs.

A mother who has ample resources invites her daughters and daughter-in-law to a spa for a long weekend each winter. Another organizes a big city visit each year, and yet another plans a tennis trip. A woman with few resources who is a whiz in the kitchen arranges pre-holiday cook-ins and sends her girls home with great food for the freezer. One woman who lives within thirty minutes of four of her five children and step-children, and yet finds it difficult to find time together, has hired an executive chef once a quarter to do a family gourmet cooking lesson and meal. "This has been successful beyond my best hopes. Everyone in the family really looks forward to these evenings." In another family, all the men do a football weekend each year. Others organize an all-siblings camping trip late each spring. If something derails some or all the participants from coming one year, they lock in for sure on the next year.

Perhaps, you want to pick one afternoon or evening each year when after a meal, each family member does a catch up and fills the others in on work and plans for the future. Maybe your family wants to talk about best and worst of the year, the challenging athletic feat, the most interesting book, or the best meal ... whatever reflects the predilections of that group. Be careful though. If your family is a crew of jocks, and the talk is always sports, and then a couch potato joins the fray, he or she may feel like an outlier. Everyone wants to feel included.

We can ask new members of the family if there is something from their own traditions they want to bring with them. For example, some families always do ham for Easter. Others do turkey. If you are in the pork camp, and a new son-in-law comes from the poultry camp, maybe you could just go for broke and have both on the table. If his family Christmas trees are always red and silver and hers are always handmade ornaments, it might mean two trees or alternating trees. Suppose you are meat and potatoes people, and you acquire a vegetarian tofu sort. No snide cracks. No teasing, fun as it may be. The intention is to help this person feel like family, not like the outsider.

It helps to understand that we can continue to observe long-held family traditions if we are willing to be flexible about when we do it. Maybe Thanksgiving has to be celebrated every other year on the first Saturday of December or after the last football game of the year. What matters is that we come together and share a good time. Does it really matter that it match the highlighting on the calendar? One woman told me that her whole family has ended up celebrating Tooth Tuesday, the day the oldest grandchild lost his first tooth. It started as an accident, and now it's a habit.

When we live far from our children, having visits tied to the calendar can make it easier for everyone to plan. Parents always visit on Memorial Day or the first weekend in the spring or for Halloween. The grandchildren come the second week of June for ten days—until they get old enough for soccer camp and that stops working. Sometimes our children give us bad news a bit brusquely.

"Sorry Mom, the kids can't come this year. Hope you are okay. Gotta go." It may be that they are, in fact, insensitive, or it may be that they feel bad letting us down and are afraid we are going to make them feel worse. Or maybe they have no idea what the visit means to us. Sometimes, we just have to find someone else's children to nurture to meet the need we have in us when our own children are unable to satisfy it.

And then there is the other side of this. Our children want us to continue to do what we have always done: cook an elaborate meal with three desserts, decorate the entire house, construct a haunted house, and we, wanting still to make them happy, keep doing it when it has long stopped being something we want to do. One woman, musing on just such a dilemma, suddenly imagined a strategy she might try. "I think next Easter, I am going to get a baton and decorate it with family pictures and, after dinner, I am going to introduce the passing of the baton ceremony and explain that this is my last year for doing this. It's time someone else took the baton, and I'll help. I can still do the desserts ... just not the rest of it."

The term new tradition has contradiction built in. Tradition is something we have done before, and new is the opposite. I believe we get new traditions by using the threads of the past and reweaving them in ways that meet current needs, or by looking to the traditional emotions we hope to evoke but creating family activities that work in untraditional circumstances. Perhaps, we loved Christmas, but our son-in-law is a Muslim. We always went to football games, but now we or they have to work on weekends. It's lovely to have family rituals that are repeated every year. But *What are we supposed to do?* is not nearly as helpful a question as *How do we want to feel?* and then *What can we do that will give us that feeling?* Forget the shoulds and oughts, and focus on the cans and wills. Change is the most constant of constants. 🍃

CHAPTER TEN

Older Still

❧

"BE KIND TO THE PEOPLE WHO WILL CHOOSE YOUR NURSING HOME."

– Bumper sticker seen in California

Twenty years ago, shortly after we moved to Houston for my husband's work, my stepfather died, and my mother moved here as well. She moved into a light and spacious apartment building with sixty-three units near the Galleria. The other day, I was visiting her, and as I walked from my car toward the front door, a woman from the building was coming out in a wheelchair with an attendant. My mother is also now in a wheelchair, and it clobbered me to realize that when I first started coming to this building, my mother and her peers looked like me. They zipped in an out, wearing smart outfits and cute shoes. They had good haircuts and cheerful smiles and dashed here and there in their cars. Somewhere along the line, my mother and others as well started carrying canes, but they were hardly slowed. Some time later, I noticed a proliferation of walkers. Now, I see attendants and wheelchairs.

I wonder if I am looking at my own future. Will I go from zippy to droopy? Are these women foreshadowing my fate? If they are … if they are … I struggle to get my mind around this thought … if they are, what does it mean to me, for me? Do I want to think about this? Can I prepare for it? Should I just go buy another pair of cute shoes? I do not want to dread old age or fear dying. This is destiny. We are all dying, and it is inescapable. The focus, of course, must be on living, on having as satisfying a time as possible for as long as possible.

One joy of this stage in my life is my children and their wives. I love the times we are together. I love it when they send a perfect gift—headphones to wear at the gym or the compelling novel to read on a plane—and when I can find just the right cookbook, tech gadget, etc., to send to them. I like watching them unfold their own lives. Being with my children and their children is a call to life, to doing and being and growing.

But there is a dark side as well which is called up for me by the decline of the women in my mother's building. Now, I can join my children swimming or walking, playing Scrabble, arguing politics. I can roll on the floor with a grandbaby. I can cook for a dozen without difficulty. But I suspect there will be a day when I cannot … cannot, perhaps, roll on the floor or even walk, when I cannot cook and take little pleasure in playing competitive games and arguing politics. What if, against all hope, the future brings circumstances I cannot handle alone? I want to believe my family will be there to help. It isn't death I worry about. It's that an awkward space between fully living and fully dying might occur. I want the ties that bind to be tight in the good times so they hold in the hard times.

What Will I Want?
The day our first grandchild was born in Boston, we were in California. My mother, then ninety-two, was in Houston. That evening, as my husband and I were celebrating over a late dinner, my cell phone rang. My mother told us she was "feeling odd," and she thought maybe this was it, the end was at hand for her.

Happily, it wasn't, but it was a difficult evening. A few weeks later, when we went to visit this new grandchild, I was telling our son about his grandmother, revived but recalcitrant. I complained that she didn't want to do things I thought she should be doing. I thought she needed to go back to working with a physical therapist. I thought she needed to come with me to the audiologist to see if we couldn't get a newer hearing aid that gave her a little more juice. I thought she needed to stop waiting to die and figure it might take a while, and find ways to make life more interesting. I thought she needed to make the effort to dress and go out more. I complained that she ignored all my good advice.

As I wound down with my complaints, my son asked me a question that stopped me cold and grabbed so hard, it still reverberates. "Mom," he asked, "how do you want me to treat you when you are old like Nana?" When he asked that question, my mother, his grandmother, was living independently, driving, managing her life. After her moment of panic, she continued on in that way until the very end of that year when she fell down in her kitchen, broke no bones, but deeply injured her spirit and lost all her "stuffing." Her mind was intact, but, overnight, she became an invalid, unable to walk or care for herself. And so, I discovered, my husband and I were going to learn the last chapter of our relationship with my mother, a chapter in which her need for us would be far more acute, and our experience in addressing her problems was nil. My mother-in-law had lived in a different city. My husband's brother was the responsible child, and we sat on the sidelines. Now it was our turn.

Until now, the focus of these chapters has been on what *we* can do to have a good relationship with our children. Here we confront the shift we all hope to avoid. Now we are talking about how, when we are no longer vigorous, our children should behave with us. Yet, as this chapter unfolded, it became clearer and clearer to me that even in the closing act, if we have the good luck to remain of sound mind, we must remain responsible for our own attitude. What I want to say to my son is that I will age, and it may be difficult, difficult for both of us. But it is my life, and I will learn to accept what this life brings, whether I like it or not. And he must accept it, whether he likes it not. If I or his father face difficulties, I hope both of our sons will stand with us in facing those problems but not believe it is their job to fix the problems. My mother keeps teaching me that she is going live her own life, even in difficult days.

Since I am not yet aged—at least sixty-five isn't feeling old today—I don't really know how I will feel should I move into my eighties, maybe my nineties. But, as our son pointed out, it is useful to contemplate in advance since we don't know when the need will arise. My own mother's answer, " … just mind your own business and don't tell me what to do; I just want to see how you feel at ninety …," hasn't felt right on the receiving end today, but there may be more wisdom in her words than I can hear. It is impossible for me to know how she feels and what she really needs. My need to "fix" my mother is clearly not aligned with her need. What my mother is teaching me, and what I hope my children may come to learn, is that I cannot "fix" her, and they will not be able to "fix" me. While I want to hang on to the illusion of control, the idea that I can control my aging, I am beginning to suspect this is, indeed, an illusion.

The Careful Considerations of Friendship

I don't know how I will feel about these words in twenty years, but I'm formulating an answer to my son for now that balances family and friendship. I understand my children are not my friends, that our relationship is that unique connection between parent and child. But there is a way in which we are candid and honest with close, old friends yet show a carefulness, a respectfulness that can be forgotten with parents. As soon as we begin to feel superior to a friend, the nature of the friendship shifts.

With my most valued friends, there is mutual respect and mutual trust. We do give each other advice. Eva is my source for how to do a better job with makeup, which after fifty years of work, I still don't have right. And she is a master at reframing, at helping me see an issue from a different angle that changes my point of view. Sue keeps me from saying things I know I shouldn't say. Barbara reminds me that the faults I had at twenty are still operative, and I need to watch for them. But they do this with such good spirit, with such kindness, and with an understanding that I may once again ignore their advice, as they often do mine, and we will still find each other worthy companions. They don't tell me what to do. They tell me what they would do and why.

What I like about these three friendships is that when we see the world differently, we talk about it. Barbara will say, "Look, think about it this way ... do you think it is possible you are resisting because ... Are you going to get what you want if you do that ...? And I find myself getting clearer from the conversation. Sue will say, "Oh, yes, you should certainly say what's on your mind like that ... You will feel so much better ... for five minutes. Of course, it won't work and will backfire, and then you will feel so much worse, but then you can call me again." And I laugh and am cured.

Because my friends are willing to have me ignore their best advice, and because they know that even when I don't do as they say, I am not an idiot, we remain friends. I want my children to give me their best advice, to tell me why they think what they do and where they think I'm misguided ... but I want them to do so with respect and with no expectation that I will do what they say because they say it. Dr. Robert Reichlin, a Houston psychologist specializing in geriatrics, believes children must assume the parent knows what is best for himself or herself. Until there is evidence of mental incompetence, children should work on the assumption that the parent needs to set the terms. Maybe my mother is right. Maybe being ninety makes it harder to do things than I understand.

We so often feel a license to say things to parents and children we wouldn't say to others. We aren't dishonest with our friends, not so careful that the friendship feels patronizing or inauthentic. We speak candidly, but we have boundaries. It is that kind of care I wish my sons to take with me, just as I am reminding myself to take the same kind of care with them.

I want to tell my sons: I am going to die. The longer it takes, the more I will age, and aging often brings losses with it. Expect this. Understand it is a natural occurrence. I can't help it, and neither will you when the moment is yours. I come to this from an understanding that my mother's aging makes me angry. When she is slow or forgetful or stubborn, I lose patience in ways I don't with others. I am not, I understand, angry with her but with the situation, with having to watch my own mother decline when I want her to be the woman I knew at twelve and twenty-two and even forty. And I get fussy sometimes with her because I feel guilty. Objectively, I am a good daughter. Subjectively, I always feel there is more I could and should be doing, and when I decide not to do it, it can make me grouchy with my mother. I would love to avoid this with my own children. I don't want them to find themselves feeling guilty. I do hope they can be there for me when I really need support. But how much is enough? Oh my lord, who can answer that? It is the other side of the question: How much is enough to do for our children?

The Quality of the Conversation

I like what James Hillman, the Jungian psychologist, writes in his book, *The Force of Character: And the Lasting Life.*

> Physiology—the brain, the circulation, the joints— remains undeniably important, but as an explana- tory model for understanding later life it declines

in power. Its explanations limp; its insights dim. It can't tell us enough...When the paradigm shifts, the question "What is healthy for my nature?" is transformed into "What is important for my character?" ... Values come under more scrutiny, and the qualities such as decency and gratitude become more precious than accuracy and efficiency.[1]

I want, with all my heart, for my sons to act as if this were true. I want them to know that it is quite possible to have limbs that limp and backs that bend and be dancing the tango with sexy grace in my spirit. Heed Hillman's observation:

"In old age, interest shifts from information to intelligence. By this I mean that information brings news, while intelligence searches for insight."[2]

Dr. Reichlin, the Houston psychologist, notes that aging means eventually realizing we do not have to keep up in order to go on. Rather we may move in whatever directions are meaningful and satisfying for us. Urging my mother to do the things I think she should do feels "right," but, in fact, I see that it can be "wrong." Rather, my role now is to help her do what she wants to do as best I can.

What Kinds of Dividends?

I want to remind my sons that I didn't spend all that time doing things for them so they could "pay me back" when I am old. Yes, there is a generational sense of responsibility that I hope they will embrace. We care for our children because they are our children. We care for our parents because they are our parents. It is part of what makes us family in community. I want my children to do what they reasonably can and then be at peace. I have led a rich and rewarding life. I don't want my aging to curb my children's opportunity to do the same.

I was talking this over with Simone, an exceptionally thoughtful woman who teaches ethics to business students and also is the major caregiver for an eighty-five-year-old mother she adores, who is dealing with cancer.

> My old, sick dog taught me so much about caring for
> my mother ... In what were Lady's final two years, she
> became stone-deaf and somewhat vision-impaired
> ... I had to learn a completely new way to commu-
> nicate with my dog, who could not respond to my calls
> or see me if she were too far away in the yard ... I real-
> ized I was more patient and understanding with my
> dog some days than I was with my mom. I never got
> out of sorts with the dog.

Simone was able to accept her dog's aging with more equanimity than her mother's. She met the dog where it was and adjusted
to its needs with no expectations that the dog could get a better hearing aid.

The Tension of Resistance and Acceptance
More important than what I want my children to do is what I can—
and cannot—do for myself as I grow older still. Can I remember my
mother and the physical cost to her of not working at keeping her
body strong and flexible? Can I remember what happens when, faced
with a steep learning curve and no external forces that say,
"Climb," we simply stop climbing, and the brain stops making
new synapses or whatever it does to stay, like the rest of the body,
limber and strong?

Technology offers a great window on the learning challenge.
There are things I don't know how to do and don't make an effort
to learn because, say I, I just really don't need to use them. Do I
really need a Blackberry or a TIVO? The answer, for me, is no,
I don't *need* the Blackberry or the TIVO, but I do need the exercise of taking on the difficult and mastering it for the sake of the
challenge. If not a TIVO, then something else.

And then, after my inspiring list of self-improvements in the
service of staving off decline, can I grasp the fact that decline may

be inevitable, and that it must be accepted just as I accepted sleep-less nights with babies or temperamental surges with teenagers?

One of the things I have so loved about my mother is that she never made me feel bad when I went out of town, when I was too busy to come by, when I had to put off an errand she has requested. She was always appreciative of what I did and didn't complain. Her cheerfulness made it easy to be with her. Other daughters have spoken of mothers and mothers-in-law who whine, berate, complain, and judge. And they don't want to be with them. Kindness begets kindness. I should stencil it on my glasses.

When the children were young, and my husband and I faced difficult moments—worrying over an unexpected bill, struggling with some challenges at work, being scared by a health issue—we protected them from our worries. I see that my mother still protects me by not sharing all her fears, all her aches, all her worries. In theory, I want to say I'm here for her, and she need-n't do this ... but she is right. Children don't appreciate our role as parents fully until they parent. They won't grasp aging fully until they age, and it is our work to do for ourselves. But as we loved them and stood by them even in their most difficult childhood moments, so may they return the favor.

Sometimes parents need children even when they were not loving and helpful parents. When I was younger, I spent a summer with the Experiment in International Living with a wonderful family in Tuscany. I am still good friends with Sophia, the daughter, a few years younger than I. She visited recently and told me a story I had not heard. Sophia's father-in-law liked Sophia's mother, a vivacious, vibrant woman. The families spent time together at family gather-ings. Over time, Sofia's mother-in-law decided that her husband and Sofia's mother were having an affair. There was no truth in this suspicion. For a variety of reasons, the charge was not even plausi-ble. No one else in the family gave it any credence, but the woman was convinced and insisted on talking about it to her son and Sofia. These false charges were so hurtful and malevolent that they caused all shared family events to cease. Sofia stopped visiting her in-laws.

She told her husband he must see his mother alone. Years later, Sofia's parents were dead, her father-in-law was dead, and only this mother-in-law remained. She became quite ill with cancer. It was Sofia who cared for her, who visited her each day, who cooked for her and bathed her. "She is the mother of my husband. She is the grandmother of my children. She was sick. She was mentally sick when she made this trouble, and then she was physically sick in her last years, and I had to help." I admire Sofia for this, for her generous spirit, for her compassion, for her sense of responsibility. I want my children to have these qualities—but I also want to have them myself as I age.

Some of you may have read about Jill Bolte Taylor, a neuroanatomist who was working at Harvard when, in 1996, she had a stroke in the left lobe of her brain, the side where ego, analysis, judgment, and context reside. While the stroke brought intense pain and severe losses that took years to overcome, it also brought Dr. Taylor into a world of magnificent energy. "The energy of my spirit seemed to flow like a great whale gliding thought a sea of silent euphoria."[1] Taylor, as a trained brain scientist, was able to watch herself slide between her left brain and her right brain, nd when the left brain declined, to hold onto her stunning awareness that " ... we are all part of the same magnificent field of shimmering energy ..." The New York Times review of her book notes that "Dr. Taylor shows the less mystically inclined ... that this experience of deep contentment is 'part of the capacity of the human mind.'"[3]

What comes to me in this sandwich space between my children and my mother is a curiosity about learning how to move more consciously from my strong and active left brain to my collaborative, harmonic right brain, to move away from seeing separateness with my children to seeing wholeness. I am not speaking of inappropriate dependency, of inserting myself in their lives instead of leading my own, but rather of going beyond right and wrong, fair and unfair, kind and unkind to a mellower, softer place that knows we are all doing the best we can and that applauds our good impulses rather than scoring points for execution.

This chapter is about aging, not dying, but in the course of working on it, I came across a book by Virginia Morris called *Talking about Death Won't Kill You*. It is exceptionally well written and thought provoking. It speaks to the need to discuss death and dying issues with family members while we are healthy. I recommend Morris' book to readers who want to become clearer about the process of dying, a process we will all experience.

CHAPTER ELEVEN

The Younger Generation Speaks Up

"MOM, YOU AREN'T LISTENING TO ME!"

– My sons

As I approached the end of this book, I invited my daughters-in-law to read the manuscript and let me know if there was anything they thought I ought to change or any comments they wished to make. The conversations that followed led me to decide to add a final chapter to this book, a chapter that captures the viewpoints of sons and sons-in-law, daughters and daughters-in-law.

When I first started on this project, I assured my sons and their wives that I was not writing about them. The book, I said, is from the mother-in-law perspective. It is about mothers and mothers-in-law and written for them to read. It is not a book for our children or about our children. "But you can't write a book about being a mother-in-law and not be writing about us," one of them said. "When I tell my friends my mother-in-law is writing a book about mothers-in-law and daughters-in-law, they say, 'Wow, what awful thing did you do?'"

Nothing awful! If you have read this far, you know the respect, admiration, and affection I have for my sons and their wives—and that doesn't keep me from having my own needs, fantasies, hopes and fears. But perhaps, even in a book for us, sons and sons-in-law, daughters and daughters-in-law deserve to have their point of view more in evidence. Of course, I asked my family if they wanted to write pieces, and they all turned me down cold. So instead, I threw myself on the mercy of strangers and semi-strangers.

In writing this book, I worked to interview as many mothers-in-law as I could and to look for all kinds of women across the country. Interviews with the younger generation were not nearly as organized. They were unplanned conversations that came my way rather than my looking for them. I didn't try to represent a broad cross section of those being mother-in-lawed.

When I decided to add this last chapter, just a few weeks before deadline, and I went looking for voices of the younger generation, I did so in a random but intensive search, e-mailing everyone I knew and asking them to e-mail every one they knew. I tried to take advantage of the Web and mothers' blogs, and my children's friends and the friends of my children's friends. My instructions were general: " … tell what isn't always spoken aloud. I'm looking for the good, the bad, the normal tensions between generations."

Asking people busy juggling jobs and children and mothers-in-law to stop and write an essay on demand about what they would like to say to their mother-in-law is not a great strategy for generating high volume. However, in some magical fashion, essays did arrive in my computer inbox, and I found myself falling in love with them all. The voices seemed true and heartfelt. The wish to be loved, respected, and trusted to make good decisions appears again and again, the same wishes that mothers-in-law have.

Here, in no particular order, are fourteen essays that come from all kinds of men and women. While I have done some minor editing, what you read is pretty much what I read when I opened the e-mails arriving from people I mostly did not know.

MOM, THANKS BUT *ENOUGH*

Dear Mom (in-law),

Thank you for raising such a beautiful, capable, and wonderful daughter! I am blessed that she chose me to be her husband, and so grateful to you both for everything you went through to get her to the point where she was ready to start her own life with me. However, I need you to understand that you are done raising her, and that she has started her new life with me.

My wife and I have our own priorities and hopes and dreams, and what we want from our life is different than what you wanted from your life when you and Dad first started your family. We are going to do things differently—sometimes because we're aware of some of the mistakes you made and want to avoid them; sometimes because we have opportunities you didn't have. That doesn't mean we don't value your insight or guidance; it just means that we aren't kids any more. Your daughter is not your little girl any more.

When Dad walked her down the aisle and gave her away, that was supposed to be when you acknowledged that she was an adult now who no longer needed your daily guidance or instruction. Your blessing on our marriage was supposed to be your signal to us that you trusted us to find our own way—or to ask for help when we needed it. But it's painfully obvious that you haven't yet really given her away, nor do we really have your trust.

Please, Mom, stop being a mom. Let your daughter be her own person and make her own decisions and decide what she wants from life—and let us decide where we want to go. We promise to ask for your advice and help when we need your wisdom, but the passive-aggressive, backhanded, under-your-breath accusations, and behind-the-back questioning of every move we make has to stop. Your job as a mother is finished—and twenty years of it were good and well done.

The last eight years of mothering, however, has been totally unnecessary, oppressive, and hurtful. We have three decades of life, love, and adventure to look forward to before we get to where you are in life. What we'd like more than anything is for you to encourage us to explore, enjoy, and experience it to its fullest along the way...

Sincerely,
Your son-in-law.

This piece was written by at twenty-eight-year-old man who works in software technology. He has been married seven years and is the father of two children. He currently lives in Canada.

IT IS TIME FOR YOU TO FOCUS ON YOU NOW

My mother-in-law is the most caring, most humble and hard-working person I have ever met. She was raised in a wealthy family where she didn't have to lift a finger. She married an army officer and had six children. When she carried her third child, all of her properties were taken, and her husband was put in prison as South Vietnam fell. From a woman who didn't know how to cook and never had to work in her life, she began to learn how to cook and walked for miles to work to earn less than minimum wages to feed her young children. She devoted all of her life to her husband, her sons, her daughters, sons-in-laws, and now her grandchildren.

She never stops thinking and caring about her husband, her children, their spouses, and her grandchildren. Her love shows through the daily meals she cooks for her family. She knows each of our likes or dislikes. She doesn't just cook one or two courses. She has at least four-course meals on the table every day to make sure all family members get what they like. She unites her family by reminding us of each other and hosts family gatherings. When I gave birth to my child, she took weeks of unpaid vacation to take care of me and my child. She did the same thing for her two other daughters-in-law. To me, all of her actions show an unconditional love.

Because she loves and cares too much, she always tries to protect her family and worries about every little thing. She doesn't want to travel because she is afraid no one would cook and care for her children, even though they are all grown-up now. When her youngest son expressed his interest in going to The University of Texas (UT) for a college education, she didn't want him to go because she was afraid he couldn't take care of himself. She didn't want her youngest daughter to date her same-age boyfriend because she feared he was not mature enough to take care of her daughter. In her daughter's second year of college, my mother-in-law felt afraid her daughter couldn't handle college. She asked her daughter to a take a hair beautician license so that she would have less stress. My mother-in-law calls us every week to ask us to come to her house for dinner.

Her youngest son ended up at UT; her youngest daughter, who became engaged to her same-age boyfriend, earned a bachelor's degree, and worked at a well-known public company. The message that I would like to send to my mother-in-law is that we all love her, and we feel her love. She needs to live for herself and not worry so much about us. We are all grown-up, and we know how to take care of ourselves.

The author of this piece immigrated from Vietnam at sixteen. She graduated from college with a B.A. and works as a senior accounting executive at an energy company. She is midway through a master's degree in finance. Her husband recently finished a master's degree in math and teaches math at a community college. Neither spoke English when they arrived in the United States. They have a five-month-old daughter.

THANK YOU FOR YOUR KINDNESS
AND GENEROSITY

My mother-in-law has been kind to me from the first day. We were home from our Peace Corps assignment for a wedding when she gave me a baby picture of my husband. I took it to mean she understood we were headed to marriage.

Initially my mother-in-law always seemed worried that she would be offending me and my husband by being too intrusive in our lives. She's always given us our space and never made us feel guilty about living far away or making any of the decisions we've made, although I suspect she's not been happy with all of them.

My mother-in-law, who earns a substantial amount of money, is incredibly generous with us without ever making us feel indebted. I appreciate that, but I especially appreciate that she also shows a healthy respect for how hard most people work for their money and has never made me feel bad for the amount of money we make (we're teachers, and currently I'm staying at home with the children). I think this comes from her midwestern upbringing, the daughter of a steel mill worker. My husband's brother and sister have, on occasion, made disparaging comments about our economic status that have hurt our feelings. My mother-in-law has always defended us and shown respect for what we do.

While I feel completely comfortable with her, I have never felt comfortable with my in-laws' circle of friends. I grew up in a middle-class midwestern family. When we first came home from the Peace Corps, we stayed with my in-laws for a week in their affluent California community. I was stunned by the amount of money women spent on things that seemed really silly and the way some of them spoke about Blacks, Hispanics, and women. Some of her friends threw an engagement party for us. I remember watching the men and women separate like oil and water and awkwardly following the women. The conversations revolved around jewelers and gossip about rich friends. I had absolutely nothing to say. At the meal, one husband began telling me how to be a "proper wife and hostess" by making sure I kept note of what each guest drinks and having the drinks ready for them the next time they visited. I imagine my jaw was on the table.

The only time my kind mother-in-law ever made me feel bad—and she would be horrified if she knew this upset me—was a comment she made after we moved out of California because it was too expensive for us. We wanted a community that could offer more to a family of modest income like ours and allow me to stay at home with the children. (That still stuns her.) She was visiting once, and my husband asked if she would consider moving to where her daughter lived in another California town. Her answer was, "Oh no, I love my work too much. I mean, I like to babysit the grandchildren sometimes, but let's face it, taking care of kids is not rocket science."

Staying home with the kids, as you know, is a subject of much debate, and we women can beat up on ourselves quite enough as it is. I felt pretty lousy after hearing a disparaging comment like that. She may have not intended it that way, but it made what I do now seem not as important as working for money. But I have great respect for my mother-in-law, and as the daughter-in-law, have the insecurity of feeling the need to earn her respect. So, I probably read into that comment too much!

The author of this piece is a thirty-seven-year-old mother of two, married to a teacher.

FINDING OUR BOUNDARIES

When my husband and I married, my stepson was two-and-a-half. Five months later, we were pregnant with our next son. When he was born, he was mine, my baby, and my boy. I was newly married and didn't understand the extreme importance of boundaries. Boundaries are critical to establish in the beginning of a marriage, and we learned that quick. When my mother-in-law would come for a visit she would enter the house saying, "Where is my baby, let me hold my baby," and it would drive me up the wall. "*He was mine,* and I am the parent," was how I was feeling. She was very close to her son, and I think she had that longing still to "mother" him. Knowing she couldn't, I think she assumed she could "mother" my son.

As time went on, I grew more and more frustrated with her and how she would push her way around and assume so much and not ask my permission. She would give permission to my kids to do something that I didn't allow or approve of. Finally after venting to my husband, he confronted his mother and she stopped. Every now and then she will cross the line, but my husband is not afraid to confront the situation.

I think there is something unique for mothers of sons. Sons, once they are married should defer to their wives, and she should be his focus. His mom is no longer number one, and I think that is a very hard concept for mothers of sons to grasp. I think it can cause resentment and tension.

A wise woman once painted this picture for my husband and me: When we are born, we are born in our family circle, mother, father, and children. It is the same way with your spouse—mother, father, and children in their family circle. Then once marriage happens between the two adult children, they now have *their* own circle and the mothers are *not* in it. It's only them, their spouse, and children. However, the adult son or daughters are still in their parents circle. It's a hard part of the letting-go process that is tough to swallow for many in-law parents ... But it's an important concept to be understood for in-law relationships to work well.

As the years have gone on, I have enjoyed my time with my mother-in-law more and more. I have made a concerted effort to call her, send her cards, take her to lunch, and spend quality time together. I love having her tell me stories of when my husband was growing up. I figure we are in each other's lives for a long time; I need to invest in the relationship. Is there one thing I would like to tell mothers-in-law? To never give *any* advice unless asked!

Today my mother-in-law and I have a wonderful relationship, and we know our boundaries. The older she gets, the more grace, love and appreciation I have for her.

The author of this piece is a thirty-eight-year-old mother of four—a stepson nineteen, niece sixteen, son fifteen, and daughter twelve. She and her husband own a roofing company, and he is also an associate pastor. They have been married seventeen years. The author has returned to school to become a registered nurse.

NOT FINDING BOUNDARIES

Here are a few suggestions from my personal experience with my mother-in-law:

1. Refrain from purchasing and or giving negligees to a daughter-in-law on her wedding night, especially hand-me-downs from your wardrobe.

2. Do not insist that a daughter-in-law sell her home so another home with a downstairs master can be purchased to ease visiting.

3. Say thank you for a picture of the grandmother and baby sent by a daughter-in-law, even when you think the picture is not flattering.

4. Remember that when you are welcomed to visit for four to five days, it is not acceptable to make the ticket for ten days just because it pleases you, nor to request the furniture be moved out of the living area for a hospital bed because the assigned room does not have a TV.

5. This is a big one. Do not visit for Thanksgiving and insist that you and your aide will cook dinner, especially on the daughter-in-law's *first* Thanksgiving at her home. When politely declined, it is better not to order-in because you are sulking and do not like salt and pepper in your food.

6. When your daughter-in-law has a baby, do not call or visit for at least two weeks.

7. Do not call on the weekend or weekday more than once.

8. Do not e-mail every single dreadful finding about pregnancy on the Web to your pregnant daughter-in-law.

9. Never tell a daughter-in-law what *not* to do with the couple's baby during the first six months.

10. Do not give a gift and expect your daughter-in-law to praise you with thanks over and over and over for years to come.

... ...

Who really knows why my mother-in-law acts this way. The issue is that she does. Perhaps a little egocentric? A little controlling? Someone who does not respect others' boundaries?

Fortunately, my husband supports me 100 percent. He respectfully tells her to back off and allows me to run my own home. I am number one to him, and we always discuss what we want and what we expect together. We stick to our beliefs no matter what. I could see how a husband who does not support his wife could really cause harm to a marriage. This is why I would never marry someone who has not cut the cord with his mother. My son, who is a one-year-old, means the world to me. When he finds someone special, I will respect her and go out of my way to do this for him.

I do respect my mother-in-law and like her most of the time. The funny thing is that I know she does love me and thinks highly of me. How do you tell your mother-in-law that she bothers you without hurting her?

It usually takes a week or so to get over things she does, but I do get over it. I do not think she understands how her actions seem disrespectful. I simply tell myself this is more of a reflection of who she is than what she thinks of me.

Being married and having a mother-in-law has me made me become closer to my mother. My mother's annoying habits seem minimal in comparison to my mother-in-law's.

The author of this essay identifies herself as anonymous, mother of two.

YOU HAVE NO IDEA
HOW VULNERABLE I OFTEN FEEL

In thinking about my relationship with my mother and mother-in-law, I have come to understand that part of what happens is about me and my feelings of inadequacy in new roles, but it is when I am feeling my most vulnerable that I most need kindness and support. With that in mind, here are some things I want to say—but don't:

1. Please, mothers and mothers-in-law, hold back with advice and suggestions. You forget how much pressure it is just being a parent of young children. As parents, we are aware that we are not perfect—and we want to be. Maybe your advice is good, but usually, it just isn't heard. All I can hear when even my father-in-law gives advice is this: "I noticed that you need advice." That feels hurtful, distancing, like I don't measure up.

Here's an exercise we all need to practice: Notice how many times our words are judging ones.

2. My mother has a habit of adding, "...which I think is great," to the end of too many sentences regarding my children. If it's meant as support, it doesn't come across that way. It comes across as, "which I approve of, and my approval is of great importance, and you should make it central to try to earn it." When we left our daughter with a sitter it was, "Oh, you are going out to dinner, and the baby is staying with a sitter, which I think is great." It's irritating. It's a bit condescending. Wouldn't it be kinder to just say, "Enjoy your evening." And say it with a smile?

3. I think there are some things that mothers and mothers-in-law have forgotten since they were on our end. Here are a few:
   — How scary this time is—Will I ever be as good as even this person who I thought was decent but is seasily surpassable.

— The constant cultural message that it's the parents' fault if things are not terrific. There is huge pressure to be this superlative parent.

— The lack of time young couples have to talk quietly and be alone.

— Understanding that most of what is happening has nothing to do with them, but when they are defensive or insecure with us, it bubbles into something.

4. I've noticed that my own relationships with my mother and my mother-in-law have changed since we had our first child. At first there was the phase of—for lack of a better word—territory squabbles. For example, my child-rearing book vs. their ideas and experience. It felt like there were lots of issues. I was insecure about what I was doing. And how could it be any other way? What prepares you for this total shift to becoming a parent? When the mothers thought there was a better way, it made me feel awkward and inexperienced, and I got defensive.

After we got our sea legs, I grew so much closer to my parents of all types. I was more relaxed about not being perfect. I was able to admire things in them even while I saw their flaws. Issues came and went more naturally. Things didn't become so big.

I think it's really important to bend your knees in this process, in-laws. Wait five years after your grandkids are born before you label the relationships you have with your children and their spouses as problematic. There is this pupa stage that has to be undergone. If you make too many things a big deal in this time, they will remain a big deal for a long time. Have a little faith. Be extra generous. Turn the other cheek. It's a really tumultuous time for us on this end.

The author of this essay is has been married a decade to a businessman. They have two young children. She formerly worked in education and lives in a major metropolitan area.

IT *IS* POSSIBLE TO LIVE HAPPILY WITH IN-LAWS

My husband and I spent most of our married lives away from our families, so we are happy to have them directly in our lives today. We taught school across the state after graduating from university the first time, then jumped into an overseas assignment with the Peace Corps which took us to Asia for a couple of years. This time away really let us settle into our marriage, which I believe is why we were secure enough to happily move in with my in-laws when we returned stateside, and again after returning from going to graduate school and establishing careers on the East Coast.

Living in shared quarters is a balancing act at times, and you have to keep perspective on the pros and cons of the situation when you're assessing whether to pick a battle or not. When we first lived together in a modest-sized house, there were two things that made me cringe—sharing the bathroom as well as a crammed refrigerator. I always thought I'd have a problem with competitiveness (like I have with my own mom) and that we'd try to stake out territory in areas of our lives like the cooking and scheduling, but that stuff really did work itself out without any problems.

It was my in-laws' perspectives on nudity that really cramped my style. I was used to walking around in my underwear while getting ready in the morning or going to bathe—but it just took me a few times of making my mother-in-law cringingly avert her eyes to realize that robes weren't optional any more. On the flip side, she let me clean out the fridge and rearrange the shelves into a semblance of order. Luckily, our current home is more spacious, and there are plenty of bathrooms to go around. Occasionally I'll see a figure darting around the corner to get away from me when I'm undressed, but it happens pretty rarely.

Living with my mother-in-law is a pleasure because we have genuine affection for each other and are both practical people who enjoy life and appreciate the things we have in our lives. It's actually amusing how she prefaces her child-rearing advice with self-effacing statements since she successfully raised my husband, but I appreciate the tact she uses to put in her two cents because it illustrates the need families have to be polite to one another just to keep the communication system running smoothly.

She's my role model for cultivating a successful marriage because she's kept it going strong for forty-one years already. Since we've come into each other's lives, I've held her hand as her husband faced surgery for prostate cancer; she's coached me through tough times at work when I've lost perspective on the bigger picture; and we've been co-conspirators trying to manage our husbands' behaviors around the house.

We've agreed to disagree on a few things. I'm into shopping at sales and wearing things until they're tossed, and she's into buying quality at any price and keeping things forever. I'm still working on her tendency to keep things in the fridge way too long—we tease her about always saying, "But I'm going to bring that for lunch!" whenever we try to clean out the fridge. So I just wait until she's out of the house and can't catch me dumping unrecognizable leftovers into the trash.

Would I like more privacy? You bet. Would it be awesome to come home from work and just eat in front of the TV once in a while instead of sitting down to dinner as a family? Oh, yeah. But would I trade the extra set of loving hands that values my little heathens as much as I do? Or give up my morning conversations over the paper while our husbands sleep? No way.

The author of this piece is a thirty-nine-year-old nurse practitioner. Her husband is a technology professional, and they have two small children. The family lives in a semi-rural area.

LOVE WAITING TO BE SPOKEN

My mother-in-law and I have difficulty communicating. I am not referring, however, to the traditional meaning of not being understood. Rather, we literally speak two different languages. She speaks Spanish and is of Central American descent. Though I am of Mexican descent, I am a second generation Mexican-American born in the United States who learned to speak only English.

Thus, we seldom speak to each other beyond "Hola! Como estás?" This communication gap keeps us from having a close relationship, even though my wife and I have been married for ten years. Note that I do understand most of spoken Spanish, and my mother-in-law also understands much of spoken English. This is to say that we both could speak in our native tongue and the other would understand. So there exists a bridge across this chasm, if we chose to use it.

It is a convenient excuse to use the language barrier as a reason not to communicate and not to get close, not to acknowledge that we are so different, which really is the reason for the divide. She is a gregarious person who loves to talk. I am a quiet and intro-verted person. While this would seem like a complementary combination, it just amplifies our differences.

I would like my mother-in-law to know that though I have not said it, I love and respect her and appreciate the matriarchal role that she plays in my wife's family. I want her to know that I think she has done a fabulous job raising her family of four daughters and one son and how happy I am to be welcomed to be a part of her wonderful family. I want to thank her for bearing and bringing up my wife, as she is a better spouse than I deserve. I dare say proudly that I got the pick of the litter.

I'd like for her to understand that it is not that I do not want to talk to her, and that it is not an aloofness that keeps me from talking to her, but rather that it is just the way I am wired. I would like to apologize for not making a greater effort to get to know her better or just converse on the happenings of the day, because I know she would enjoy that. I am sorry that I always took the easier and lazier way of not saying anything.

One thing that I particularly admire about her is how I have heard of her objecting to something in a family member's life but then watched as she refrained from directly interfering other than to state her opinion, which is something that everyone is entitled to do. I know it is only natural for the parent to want what is best for his or her child.

I hope that she knows that I do my best to protect, care for, and love her daughter. And though I am not rich nor the best provider amongst her sons-in-law, I do think that in our house, we are happy, fulfilled, and truly blessed. I am committed to continue to do my best in that regard, come what may, though I am prone to mistakes sometimes.

I wish she was more of a fixture in our children's lives and that we all would see her more often, especially being that she is so close by. I am jealous that other grandchildren get a disproportionate share of attention from her. Although I do believe that she loves our children too, and I know that language, also, plays a role in their lack of closeness.

I am working on my Spanish in hopes that one day we will talk more and become closer. But as far as that goes, I should go ahead and say these things in the language that I know. I believe that she will understand.

The author of this piece is forty-four-year-old son-in-law who is a proud father of two and stepfather of two, born to a lower-income family in east Los Angeles, a good and quiet student, who grew up to be an information technology professional.

LOVING A STRANGER

Dear Mother-in-law,

I'm sorry we bombed your country. It must have been both awful and fascinating to see a Tomahawk missile go through your neighborhood. Knowing you were there makes military involvement far less abstract.

It's strange not having a common language. That first meeting, nearly five years ago now, was a bit tense, especially on my side. But your wonderful daughter had introduced me well, and when your father "found" that last dusty bottle of the long-lost Good Stuff in the basement, it was a favorable sign.

Your little granddaughter is learning four languages, and she's better than me in three of them; two of them, Serbian and Hungarian, are yours. You and I must communicate with signs and gestures, fragments, and expressions, and mostly indirectly through your daughter and granddaughter, my precious wife and baby. Signs of you are on them: my wife's fierce devotion to our baby, the songs she sings her, her anxiety and shyness, the baby's fascination with the phone and with flowers. You're an ethnic minority in a country that doesn't treat such people well, and I love it that my wife is passionate about defending oppressed minorities. She has your acute eye and sense of design, and the baby will, too.

You love me, mostly because of and through them. I know you are happy when I send pictures and when you are told that I am a good husband and father and make them happy. I love that too. I love that it makes you light up and greet me warmly, and send me artistic Powerpoint photo collections. I must admit I don't really know you very well, but I love you, too, and we are building a relationship at long distance, one step at a time.

The author of this piece is a research scientist, married to a woman of Hungarian-Serbian background. They have a two-and-half year-old daughter and live in the Southwest.

WHY COULDN'T SHE SEE THE FABULOUS ME?

My mother-in-law is hip. She is beautiful, talented, outgoing, and adores her children—especially my husband. I knew the mother-in-law stereotypes, but when I married I decided what was true for other people did not have to be true for me.

I desperately wanted my mother-in-law to like me. To adore me. To be friends with me. To think I was amazing and fabulous. I saw her adore her son/my husband, nearly possessive and smothering, and in some odd way hoped she would love me like that, too.

When we announced our engagement, I pretended to ignore it when she said, "She is not your type. I thought you would marry your high school girlfriend." I pretended it did not hurt. I thought if I smiled enough, worked hard enough, became a great hostess, was a fabulous wife, and the most excellent mother, that she would change her mind. She would adore me and love me like she loved her son.

During our engagement, my young sister was playing at my mother-in-law's house. She fell off the trampoline and had some minor bumps. My mother-in-law scooped my sister into her arms, dramatically hugged and kissed her all over. My sister started smiling. I stood there wondering how fantastic it would feel get all that love and attention from this woman!

A year after we married and I was accepted to graduate school in another state, my husband, with an undeclared major, and I decided to move. I pretended it did not hurt when his mom said to me, "You could be like the other wives and waitress while he finishes school."

During the entire marriage, my husband did not buy or ship one holiday card or gift. During the entire marriage, my mother-in-law consistently thanked my husband for these elaborately wrapped gifts, clever cards, and hordes of grandchildren pictures. Every. Damn. Time. After my second child was born, I stopped pretending that she did not hurt me. I started commenting that she did not, not ever, thank me for the tediously handmade gifts. I said it was odd that she called and when I answered, simply asked for her son, as if I were his secretary. My husband and I even laughed about it. My laughter was the kind that falls out when you are too proud to cry.

The last few years, our marriage saw some tough times, and we are now divorced. During this period, my mother-in-law has not made any contact with me. Not once. In the early months of chaos, I'd lay awake in bed wishing her to call me, to help me, to give some direction to the mess. The mess is now cleaned up by divorce paperwork and a custody schedule. I tell my friends I'm thrilled I'm not obliged to send her one more unacknowledged card. The truth is, I'm also devastated to have never gained her acceptance.

The author, a social worker, was married to her husband for seventeen years. They have three children, and she now lives in the far West.

A HAPPY BONDING FOR TWO INDEPENDENT WOMEN

When I first moved to Houston, engaged and a few months away from marrying my husband, I was shocked when friends or family dropped by unannounced to say hello. As a native New Yorker, these spontaneous displays of southern charm were not yet part of my hardwiring. I had lived in an apartment building all my life. There were never surprise visits since the doorman protected us all by calling to announce whomever arrived at the downstairs door. This seemed quite right for me.

My mother-in-law immediately understood my reserve. I was, again and again, touched to find small tokens of welcome at my door, gifts she left without ever ringing the bell. When I first arrived, it was a set of satin hangers and brand new, fluffy blue towels. I wanted to build a strong relationship with her, but with a busy new job at the outset of my arrival, I needed the space and time to develop my relationship with her at my own pace.

A year later when I was pregnant, she urged me to go shopping with her for maternity clothes. Still feeling my way and not at all in the mood to try on clothes, I demurred. But I was thrilled when one morning, I opened the door and hanging on the knocker were a variety of clothes. "Try them on and keep what you like; if you don't like any of them, I'll take them back," she said. After thirteen years and four pregnancies, I still remember a blue linen sleeveless dress that was my number one standby.

I have developed a wonderful relationship with my mother-in-law. I am very thankful. One reason I think it is so strong is that my husband, who married at forty-five, had already established an understanding that guided their time together. They were close, but he did not want surprise visits either, and she understood his need for privacy and independence. They did a lot together, but dates were planned in advance. Another factor in my relationship with her is that it has developed slowly and gradually, with us each respecting our individual paths to find mutual middle ground in the context of the changing events of our busy lives. My mother-in-law, who married at eighteen and had four children in six years, never held an office job, but she has always understood the importance to me of my education and my career, and has supported my various employment decisions. This has so helped our relationship.

My mother-in-law is very active with a host of friends, charitable interests, and extended family. For me and my husband, every day is a juggling act, keeping up with our four children and all that that brings with different schools, activities, and childcare issues, not to mention busy jobs. While she is always there in a pinch if necessary, taking the children to a doctor's appointment if I can't make it, I don't ask her to babysit.

She is the keeper of the family stories and the children's muse of theater and film, introducing them to the pleasures of the lights going down and the curtain going up. She loves to delight our children and surprise them with afternoons at the cinema and nights at the theater. I happily agree. I am thrilled the children are developing their own relationship with their grandmother—their only grandparent now—just as I have developed a unique relationship with her.

The author of this piece is a forty-five-year-old mother of four who lives in Houston and works as a writer and journalist.

MY TWO MOTHERS-IN-LAW

My first mother-in-law was from a Shephardic family in Constantinople, Turkey, educated by nuns and sent to New York for an arranged marriage. She and her husband manufactured women's ready-to-wear and brought up their three sons in Brooklyn. My husband, the youngest son, was the first male in his family ever to change a diaper, but he never ventured past sandwich making in the kitchen. His mother would darkly hint that she didn't mind my cooking, but my food would surely poison her husband.

This mother-in-law told me horrifying stories about her other two daughters-in-law. I'm sure she told them equally horrifying stories about me. I never fully understood her Middle-Eastern method of talking circuitously on every subject. On the good side, her hospitality was immense. She and her husband supported us while my husband went to dental school. They gave us an apartment to live in while he tried and failed to pass the California State board exams. On the bad side, her suspicious nature was malevolent. When my husband died, his mother insisted I was cheating both her and my daughter out of an inheritance. In truth, I was avoiding explaining how poor we were.

Understandably, I was terrified over meeting my second mother-in-law. She turned out to be one of the kindest people I've ever met. She and her three sisters adopted me unconditionally and made me feel that I could do no wrong from the first moment they met me. This was the most delicious feeling. When they stoutly defended me in the face of slander from my husband's ex-wife and her family, I felt not only relieved but loved.

When my mother-in-law visited Houston, I happily took her shopping for the colorful clothes she loved that she couldn't find in Buffalo, New York. I went to be with her when she was dying of brain cancer. I miss her still. She taught me how to love and it was a lesson dear beyond words.

The author of this piece is an artist living with her husband in Texas, with one child deceased and one grown child estranged. She says she definitely does not qualify as "the younger generation," but that her memories of her mothers-in-law feel quite fresh and acute.

WHY CAN'T MY MOTHER SHOW BETTER?

My mother-in-law tells me that she'd envisioned another individual as her son-in-law. But, in the next breath, she calls me her dark-haired child—all her children are blond while she, like me, is brunette. I think society's stereotype would prefer that I dwell on the former and dismiss the latter; after all, I'm not supposed to get along with my mother-in-law. When she visits, aren't I expected to play golf and avoid all but the most polite conversation? Happily, it doesn't work that way. We are more likely to bet dollars on random sporting events and visit coin-collecting shops together. In my mother-in-law, I've gained another parent. Fortunate? Unbelievably so.

In the wedding vows, after "for richer or for poorer," there is no "in the midst of family," but there should be. While my family of origin has been the source of great joys, it has also been the cause of frustrations—fights over a baby's name, "innocent" comments that double as insults, unrelenting melodrama. My wife struggles mightily to make her mother-in-law relationship work, and, unfortunately, that doesn't make the good times more fulfilling; the best she seems to get is a sense of relief if things go smoothly.

As a participant in both of these relationships, I'm troubled by the dichotomy between elation on one hand and shame on the other. I consider my mother-in-law to be an extraordinary person, but so is my mother. Why doesn't the exceptional aspect of my mother show itself more often? Does she consciously pick her moments to be friend or foe? Does she only want a relationship on her terms? Where have my wife and I fallen down on our end of the bargain? My wife and I hope to be in-laws (not outlaws) someday. What can we learn from this tumult?

Honestly, there are an awful lot of times when I really don't need the damn hassle of playing at peacemaker—at a cost to my marriage, my dignity, my blood pressure. Others must feel similarly. Still, we all persevere, invoking the sanctity of grandchildren or grasping family history as justification. And…it is worth it?

The writer of this essay is a middle-aged man with two children, a wife ("who makes other soccer dads green with envy"), and a receding hairline.

LEARNING TO IGNORE THE IRRITATIONS AND COUNT THE BLESSINGS

I really like my mother-in-law (now). In fact, I liked her right away, but our road wasn't always as easy as it is now. We speak on the phone about five times a week; she and my father-in-law (and sometimes a few other relatives in tow) visit us nearly every Sunday; she regularly picks up clothes for me or things for our house. She loves and supports us, she dotes on my children, and she genuinely wants the best for us. But of course, the story wasn't without its bumps. I had to learn a few lessons before we got to this place. Three in particular come to mind as I think back.

First, I had to learn, right off the bat while planning our wedding (that first and major tangle of needs that turn ordinary people into lunatics) what it is that I could and couldn't expect from my husband. I quickly understood that I needed to have my own relationship with her that wasn't centered on asking my then-fiancé to explain my point of view to her. He is conflict-avoidant; so is his mother. My husband would have glossed over all of my needs and well-crafted points and frustrated me to no end. I learned then and there that I needed to pick up the phone and be strong enough to say my bit, and in the process forge a new relationship, all by myself.

Second, I had to appreciate what we have in common, and I don't just mean that we both love her son. I especially came to appreciate that we both enjoy a laugh and even a dose of sarcasm in the face of uncomfortable moments. One of the main reasons she and I have done so well together is that I can joke about her "Opinions R Us"-style to her face, and she will giggle. In fact, I was "outed" by a future sister-in-law (marrying into the family), who reported to our mother-in-law that my advice to her was to let our mother-in-law always have her say, listen respectfully, and then do whatever you want afterwards. Granted it wasn't so excellent of my future sister-in-law to rat me out on that comment, but the fact that our mother-in-law loves the story and tells it to everyone is the real point.

Third, I have to remind myself that when things feel not right, it's never because of ill intent. The best example of this comes from when I was pregnant. In the early months of pregnancy, I am queasy and grumpy. My mother-in-law, with the best intentions, kept telling me (and everyone around me) that what I really needed to do was just get out more and not wallow in my discomfort. I, on the other hand, was deeply committed to spending every possible moment on the couch in comfy clothes until I felt better, even if it took forever. It was hard for me to make clear that this advice was falling on deaf ears, and, in retrospect, that bit of advice—along with other small examples, like the time she told me to move the diaper-changing station up onto a filing cabinet—are a small inconvenience for allowing someone into our lives who is generous, loyal, and helpful. I hope we stay connected for years to come.

The author of this piece is a college professor married to a research scientist. They have two young children and live in the Northeast.

FURTHER READINGS

Begley, Sharon. *Train Your Mind, Change Your Brain*. Ballantine Books, 2007.

Birkman, Roger W. *True Colors: Get to Know Yourself and Others Better With the Highly Acclaimed Birkman Method*. Thomas Nelson, 1995.

Boorstein, Sylvia. *It's Easier Than You Think: The Buddhist Way to Happiness*. Harper San Francisco, 1977.

Bridges, William. *Transitions: Making Sense of Life's Changes*. Addison Wesley, 1980.

Brizendine, Louann. *The Female Brain*. Broadway Books, 2006.

Brown, Brené. *I Thought It Was Just Me: Women Reclaiming Power and Courage in a Culture of Shame*. Penguin Group, 2007.

Carson, Lillian. *The Essential Grandparent: A Guide to Making a Difference*. Health Communications, 1996.

Doidge, Norman. *The Brain That Changes Itself*. Viking, 2007.

Erikson, Erik H., Joan M. Erikson, and Helen Q. Kivnick. *Vital Involvement in Old Age*. W.W. Norton and Company, 1986.

Ephron, Nora. *I Feel Bad About My Neck: And Other Thoughts on Being a Woman*. Random House, 2006.

Hillman, James. *The Force of Character: And the Lasting Life*. Ballantine Books, 1999.

Johnson, Sue, and Julie Carlson. *GrandLoving: Making Memories with Your Grandchildren*. Heartstrings Press, 1996.

Keirsey, David, and Marilyn Bates. *Please Understand Me: Character & Temperament Types*. Prometheus Nemens Book Co., 1984.

Kutzen, Dr. Stephanie. *Grandparenting: Tales From the Crib—When Your Children Become Parents*. Global Source Publishing, 2006.

Langer, Ellen J. *Mindfulness*. Perseus Books, 1989.

Lerner, Harriet. *The Dance of Anger: A Woman's Guide to Changing the Patterns of Intimate Relationships*. Harper Collins, 1986.

Lieberman, Susan. *New Traditions: Redefining Celebrations for Today's Family*. Farrar, Strauss and Giroux, 1991.

Morris, Virginia. *Talking about Death Won't Kill You*. Workman, 2001.

Palmer, Helen. *Inner Knowing: Consciousness...Creativity...Insight...Intuition...* J. P. Tarcher Books, 1998.

Palmer, Helen. *The Enneagram: Understanding Yourself and the Others In Your Life*. HarperCollins, 1991.

Penley, Janet and Diane Eble. *MotherStyles: Using Personality Type to Discover Your Parenting Strengths*. Da Capo, 2006.

Pearman, Roger R., and Sarah C. Albritton. *I'm Not Crazy, I'm Just Not You: The Real Meaning of the Sixteen Personality Types.* Davies-Black Publishing (United States), 1998.

Quinn, Robert E. *Change the World: How Ordinary People Can Accomplish Extraordinary Results.* Jossey Bass, 2000.

Seligman, Martin E.P. *Learned Optimism: How to Change Your Mind and Your Life.* Random House, 2006.

Siegel, Daniel J. *The Developing Mind: How Relationships and the Brain Interact to Shape Who We Are.* Guilford Press, 1999.

Tannen, Deborah. *You're Wearing That? Understanding Mothers and Daughters in Conversation.* Random House, 2006.

Tieger, Paul D., and Barbara Barron-Tieger. *Just Your Type: Create the Relationship You've Always Wanted Using the Secrets of the Personality Type.* Little Brown and Company, 2006.

NOTES

Chapter 2
1. Brown, *Just Me*, 215.
2. Doidge, *Brain That Changes*, 3–5.
3. Ibid., 59.
4. Ibid., 60.

Chapter 3
1. Tannen, *You're Wearing That?* 4.

Chapter 4
1. Siegel, *The Developing Mind*, 73.
2. Tannen, *You're Wearing That?* 105–07.

Chapter 5
1. Mireya Navarro, "My Child's Divorce is My Pain", *New York Times*, September 2, 2007

Chapter 6
1. David Brooks, "Harmony and the Dream," *New York Times*, August 12, 2008.
2. Brenda Mueller, "The Personality Page," BSM Consulting, http://www.personalitypage.com.

Chapter 10
1. Hillman, *Force of Character*, 55.
2. Ibid., 57.
3. Leslie Kaufman, "A Superhighway to Bliss," *New York Times*, May 25, 2008.